Roy

Nick

Good luck with your

goes game.

Roy Vomastek

Roy

The 78-Year-Old Champion

BRIAN MULVANEY & JAY LAVENDER

NSPYR
Charlottesville

Published in the United States by NSPYR LLC
Cover Photo by Dickie Morris
Cover Design by Albano Design & Dickie Morris
1932 Map by Jen Maton/If So INKlined Calligraphy & Design
ISBN 978-1-939495-04-4 (print)
ISBN 978-1-939495-00-6 (eBook)
NSPYR.com

For Shirley

Contents

Introduction

Part 1 by Brian Mulvaney

I grew up s bout 90 miles from Detroit in Lansing, Michigan—the state capital and proud home of Oldsmobile before General Motors shuttered the brand. My three older brothers and I were obsessed with sports, spending our summer days working in the small family store and playing baseball, then evenings with our ears glued to a small radio. We hung on every word from legendary announcer Ernie Harwell as the 1967 Tigers struggled for the American League Pennant while Motor City burned around them with racial unrest. The '67 team broke our hearts on the final day of the season but in 1968 came back to win it all creating unity amidst the continuing chaos. For a young boy like me, it was my first powerful example of how a game and athletes could impact and transform their surroundings, even if only temporarily. During the summers of 1967 and 1968, for the few hours each day that the Tigers took the field, everything stopped. Radios shared a common bandwidth as we all rooted with the same hope for our team. During those summers, my love for sport and its mysterious power was burned into my soul.

I grew up in awe of my oldest brother, John, a renowned high school pitcher who often struck out 12 to 15 hitters in a seven inning game and went on to become a successful Golden Gloves boxer. My other brothers, Jim and Ray, were also baseball players and encouraged me to play, too, but there was only one game for me. Basketball. No one else in my family had played but it was my calling and I dropped the other sports to dedicate everything to it.

My successful high school career at Lansing Everett High—which included Team Captain, Most Valuable Player, All-City and All-Conference Honors my senior year—was capped off by winning the first Class A District title in our school's history in 1974. Basketball was important to me in many other ways, helping me to overcome painful shyness and meeting my first girlfriend, a pretty cheerleader who left me tongue-tied in person though I could bare my soul over the phone. Turned out, I was better at playing basketball than dating and this first relationship lasted only two weeks. But it changed me. I loved basketball and I doubled down. It was my path, my passion and, I believed, my destiny.

One Saturday evening shortly after our championship senior season ended, I was at a party where my buddy, Larry Johnson, walked through the front door towing behind a 13-year-old who was half-a-foot taller than him.

"Hey Brian, this is my little brother, Earvin."

Earvin was going to be attending Lansing Everett High the following year and he wanted to learn about Coach George Fox, the league and the players who were returning. He wanted to know everything he could and for the next hour we talked basketball. At some point in the conversation, Larry looked at me and declared, "My brother can play. He's going to be great." And for the first time, I witnessed Earvin Johnson's smile that would one day light up the sports world and endear him to his teammates who knew him as "Buck" and to the fans who would know him as "Magic."

After high school, I grew stronger physically, developed new skills and began playing at a higher level. Following a year of junior college basketball, I transferred to Creighton University where I made the Bluejay's team as a walk-on. Competing at the Division 1 level filled me with dreams about where the game might take me. But I began to learn, painfully, that while I had the physical gifts to compete with just about anyone, I didn't have the basketball IQ for a disciplined approach to the game. I could play up-tempo, playground-style but in a system I was lost, almost always in the wrong place at the wrong time. I began to explore transferring to a couple of schools that were interested and went home to think about my next step. While there, I suffered a devastating injury in a pick-up game, severely tearing the ligaments away from the bone in my left ankle. Despite diligent efforts to rehabilitate it, I never regained form. My ankle hurt constantly and was chronically weak, remaining so today, a lingering reminder of my disappointment. I was done with basketball and the game I loved had taught me a lesson I didn't want to learn: sometimes dreams don't come true.

I was still driven, so I focused my competitive nature into completing my studies, attending graduate school and embarking on a successful business career that fulfilled dreams well beyond anything I had previously imagined. But my love of sport remained. I still followed basketball and watched as Larry's little brother, Earvin, won championships at every level. I was amazed at how he single-handedly transformed the professional game, blurring positions together—he was a 6'9" point guard one second, a power forward the next, then a center, all the while playing with the unrestrained joy of a child and the smile of that 13-year-old kid. He knew he was playing a game and loved every second of it. Watching him control the game, I wondered why I had never been able to see the court the same way. He played as if he were conducting an orchestra; I played like I was trying to find my way through a crowded lobby.

As my career consumed me, I had little spare time but still needed a physical outlet. I took up racquetball for a while, then tennis—neither provided the joy that basketball had. I played them to work up a sweat and stay in shape but I missed feeling passionate about a game. That changed when I started playing golf in my mid-40's. I'd occasionally hacked it around on the local munis when I was a kid but had never had access to instruction and lost interest. As an adult learning the game, I was instantly smitten by the beauty of golf courses, the history of the sport, the solitary-yet-social nature, the ridiculous degree of difficulty, the influence of the elements and the comical, painful and often humiliating role of luck. Thus began a new journey for me, producing many friendships and taking me to unique and beautiful places. Importantly, it gave me a second chance to love and try to understand a game completely. I had failed with my first love, basketball. I hoped to get it right with golf.

Golf is how I met Jay Lavender in December 2002. I was playing as a guest of my friend and colleague, Steve Duffy, at the Palms Golf Club in La Quinta, California. It was a busy morning so the starter suggested we join a threesome about to tee off and play as a group of five. He said they were strong players and played fast. Strong players indeed—Jay had played for Dartmouth, Dan Jennings had played for the University of Arizona and qualified for a few USGA Mid-Amateurs, and Brad Shaw was playing golf for the University of Southern California (and would later qualify for the USGA Amateur & Mid-Amateur.) Over the course of the round, we found a shared a love of the game with much to talk about. From that chance encounter, I developed three wonderful friendships that in turn lead to many new friendships as we introduced each other to our friends in golf.

One of those new friendships was with Jay's dad, Harold Lavender, or "Big H" as he is known to anyone who has crossed his path. Big H's life-long odyssey in golf had included him being the band leader of an annual trip to Scotland, England or Ireland for a small, loosely knit group of golf nuts. After Jay introduced me to his dad, I was invited to join one of his trips. It was my first journey to play true links golf and though a magnificent experience, included a humbling lesson that became the key to making sure that my love affair with golf turned out different than my experience with basketball.

We were playing at Royal County Down Golf Club in Northern Ireland on a beautiful, cool afternoon in the summer of 2006. Big H and I were having a friendly match against Jay and Phil, another member of the group. The match was close and competitive and I was engaged. I had a 5-foot putt on the final hole to tie the match. My competitive juices were flowing—I really wanted to make it. But as my putt missed left of the hole, my heart sank. Sputtering something incoherent, I apologized to Big H, whining about missing the important putt. He looked at me oddly, shook hands with Phil and hugged his son, Jay. As I walked off the green I felt a hand on my shoulder.

Out of earshot of the others Big H said to me, "Son, I really don't give a rat's ass whether you think you should have made that putt. A lot of players better than you have missed that putt on this golf course over the last hundred years or so. I'm here to have fun, play golf and enjoy the courses. Getting pissed off about it won't change the outcome." He then squeezed my shoulder and walked off.

I continued to walk, relieved my face was red from the cool wind so my embarrassed blush didn't show.

A light had gone on. I got it.

For much of that afternoon, I lost sight that I was playing a game with friends. I was too focused on the competition at the exclusion of everything else. Approaching the "important" putt as if it were a free throw to tie a game, I saw my miss only as a failure. I had missed much of the experience the day offered. The beauty, history and majesty of the setting while in the company of friends. Thinking about it later in the evening, the lesson was clear to me. It's about the moment. It's about the game. It's about the place. It's about the people. It's about competing. It's about hitting the best shot you can hit. And it's about hitting the next one. It's about all of those things, not just one of them. The moment held a mirror to my face and I knew I had to look closely at the reflection if I were to have any hope of truly enjoying the game and everything it could offer me. Someone who understood the new game I loved had shared with me something profound that I would remember forever. I didn't want to be trying to find my way through a crowded lobby with golf.

In 2008, another new world would open to me. I was blessed to be in the membership process at Crystal Downs Country Club in Northern Michigan. It was a dream come true. The magical Crystal Downs is one of my favorite places in the world and represents everything I love about golf. I had spent most of my time since my 20's living in Philadelphia and California so being able to return to my Michigan roots held even deeper significance for me. I arranged to play one day with a member, Ed Vomastek, and he mentioned that his dad was going to join us. I thought nothing more of it, looking forward to the round.

I arrived at the practice putting green outside the pro shop, shook hands with Ed and noticed a man in his mid-70's with an odd looking long-handled putter. Dressed in wrinkled khakis and a plain white golf shirt that had seen better days, an old cap slightly crooked on his head, he was standing alongside the putter, lost in his own world rolling in putt after putt. Ed called him over and introduced him to me. "This is my dad, Roy Vomastek. He's going to play with us. He's pretty good."

Roy's eyes were kind, his demeanor humble and shy. Roy shook my hand, smiled and went back to putting. A few moments later we made our way down to the first tee. While Roy rummaged through his golf bag, Ed suggested we play the back tees. I was surprised that someone over 70 years was going to play such a difficult course from the back tees but kept it to myself.

Ed offered me the honors and I hit a good drive long and down the middle. Ed teed off next, down the center then heckled his dad, "Pa, what are you doing? We need to finish before dark."

Roy looked up from digging in his bag and ambled onto the tee, driver in hand.

I can still remember watching Roy tee his ball up that first time. He seemed strong in spite of his age. When he addressed his ball, there was a sudden energy and focus. He turned back, loaded up and took a rip. Watching his ball take off like a rifle shot down the middle of the fairway, my jaw went slack.

"Where'd it go, Ed?"

"Down the middle, Pa, about 270."

Walking out of the tee box Ed turned to me and said, "We have to keep an eye on his ball. He doesn't see too well."

Walking past Roy's golf bag I saw two tags hanging from it. *USGA 2004 Senior Amateur – Bel Air Country Club –* *Contestant* and *USGA 2005 Senior Amateur – The Farms Golf* *Club – Contestant.*

I asked Ed how old his Dad was.

"76," he replied.

I quickly did the math. Roy was 72 and 73 when he had played in those Senior Amateurs.

I headed down the first fairway with a sense that I was in for a treat. Within a few holes, three things were certain...

First, I was seeing something unlike I had ever seen in my life-long love affair with sports.

Second, my journey with the game of golf was about to head down a new and interesting path.

And third, there was a story to tell.

Little did I know how special that story would turn out to be...

Brian Mulvaney
Frankfort, Michigan

Part 2 by Jay Lavender

I woke up in La Quinta, California the morning after Christmas in 2002 excited for the day ahead. I was staying with my good friends, Dan Jennings and Brad Shaw, and we were heading out to play at The Palms Golf Club. I had walked-on the Dartmouth golf team in college but Dan and Brad were far superior players and I always enjoyed playing alongside them. It was virtually guaranteed that each of them would do something memorable once a round—launch a monster drive, stuff a long-iron to kick-in range, pull off a remarkable recovery shot or go on a birdie binge.

But I don't remember a single shot either of them hit that day. I don't recall a single shot I hit either. I have no idea what anyone's score was. My lasting memory of that round is that the starter paired us on the first tee with two men I'd never met before, Steve Duffy and Brian Mulvaney.

My dad, Harold, gifted his love of golf to me. And he loves everything about the game. The history, architecture, club-making and camaraderie. He had a golf club workshop in our basement where he passed the time during the Midwest winters, the smell of burning epoxy often wafting up into the kitchen. My dad taught me how to play golf and—more importantly—taught me how to be a golfer. How to always respect the game, the course and your playing partners. He took me with him to play great courses with his friends throughout Chicago, our country, Scotland, England, Northern Ireland & Ireland. The times spent on the golf course with my dad and his friends are some of the favorite memories of my life.

When Dan, Brad, and I introduced ourselves to Steve and Brian on the first tee that December morning, even though we hadn't planned on playing with anyone else, we were friendly and respectful. We'd all spent enough time around the game to know how many friendships have started with a chance encounter on a first tee. Our five-some worked our way around the front nine bantering about life and golf, and at some point near the turn, I remember thinking to myself that Brian and I would know each other for a long time.

Over the ensuing years, as we became good friends, I discovered something else about Brian. He was a writer. I realized it first from his emails and confirmed it through our conversations. He loved to read and reflect. Learn and analyze. He was extremely observant with a quick wit. But other than the writing he had done in his business career, he hadn't ever attempted to write for others.

Writing had taken me to Los Angeles after college. By the time I graduated in 1997, I had accepted I wasn't going to make my living playing golf even though I had worked as hard as I could through college to try and reach my full potential.

I had experienced the thrill of qualifying for the Colorado & Illinois State Amateurs as well as the Illinois Open followed by the reality check of the vast difference between me and the tournament winners. Two other experiences confirmed where I stood. In August of 1995, I drove from Hanover, New Hampshire down to Newport Country Club in Rhode Island with a teammate, Steve Sugarman, to watch Tiger Woods and Buddy Marucci in the finals of the U.S. Amateur. It only took seeing Woods hit one tee shot to confirm he and I were playing a very different game. The universe made sure I got the point a month later when another teammate of mine, Dave Kantrovitz, and I were playing Canterbury Golf Club in Cleveland, Ohio on our drive back to school. After a few holes, we'd impressed our host enough for him to offer some pointed advice, "You guys better study hard, because you're not going to make your living as golfers."

Those experiences didn't keep me from dreaming but once I accepted the inevitable that I wasn't going to be more than an amateur, I was determined to find a way to earn a living that provided the time and money to play the game I loved. As I contemplated the ways I could earn a living as a writer, I discovered that most of my favorite novelists didn't publish their first book until they were in their 30's or 40's. And though I loved biographies and inspiring human interest stories, I didn't want to be a reporter. Through process of elimination—and reverse engineering the desire to be able to play golf and live somewhere warm—I set my sights on screenwriting in Los Angeles. I figured if I could get my start as a screenwriter, it would open other doors to tell more stories in other ways.

I began by writing a couple of inspiring sports dramas. *Chariots of Fire, The Natural* and *Hoosiers* were three of my favorite movies growing up and I figured if I couldn't be a professional athlete, or underdog champion, I could at least write about them. One of my first screenplays was a story about a young amateur golfer and his unlikely mentor. (Write what you know, I was told.) The script received positive attention but didn't sell. I kept writing and soon caught a run writing comedies but inspirational sports stories remained my first love.

I'd been pursuing a career as a writer for five years when I met Brian that day at The Palms. As my career progressed and I rode the roller-coaster of trying to earn a living telling stories, my friendship with Brian grew. Our shared passion for golf was the foundation for long conversations about life, business and the world and I came to value his insights. When Brian called me one day and said he had someone with an incredible story he wanted me to meet, I couldn't wait to hear more. When he told me it was a member of Crystal Downs, chills ran down my spine.

I visited Crystal Downs for the first time in September of 1996. My dad's job as a commodity trader on the floor of the Chicago Board of Trade created a network of golfers around the country and one of his friends, Jay Homan, arranged for me and my friend, Andy May, to play as his guests on our drive back to New Hampshire for our senior year. We detoured well out of our way up to Northern Michigan to see the club that my dad considered one of his favorite places on Earth. The course was practically empty when Andy and I teed off that fall afternoon as a two-some, carrying our own bags. We were absolutely mesmerized by the setting. When we finished, we were the only ones left so headed back to the first tee and hurried around the front nine again trying to outrun sunset. We putted out on our 27th hole as the sun was heading for the horizon beyond Lake Michigan and since neither of us wanted to leave, we sat down on the front bank of the 9th green to take it all in a bit longer. The course came up through my bones as I stared out over one of the most beautiful places I'd ever seen in my life. It was special day at a magical place. I hoped to be lucky enough to return.

It was over 12 years later, and five years after I first met Brian, when I drove from Los Angeles to Indian Wells, California one morning to meet Dr. Roy Vomastek and his son, Ed. We met on the range at The Reserve Club and headed out to play with Brian. I got to experience the joy of a round with Roy, watching with amazement as the old man swung driver from his heels—banging it over 270 yards—knocked his approaches on the greens and rolled his putts home side-saddle. That night, back at Brian's house, Ed said, "Pa, tell Jay your story."

For the next couple of hours I sat enthralled as Roy talked about the miracles of his life. Brian was right. There was a story to tell. But although it had a great beginning and middle, it was a story in search of its end. I told Roy I'd love to help tell his story one day and hoped to keep in touch.

I got to know him better on his subsequent trips to Southern California and my trips to Northern Michigan but was still looking for the hook when Brian left me a voicemail one Sunday morning in July of 2010, "Roy's in the finals of the club championship."

For the next few hours, I pictured Roy playing his way around Crystal Downs. I thought about his remarkable life. The uniqueness of the sport that could enable a man to turn back the hands of time for an afternoon. I tried not to get my hopes up.

And then Brian called back a few hours later with another message, "You're not going to believe this…"

He was right.

I can't believe Roy exists, that I was lucky enough to meet him and that I get to help Brian share Roy's inspiring story.

Jay Lavender
Charlottesville, Virginia

Golf is the closest to the game we call life.
You get bad breaks from good shots; you
get good breaks from bad shots—but you
have to play the ball where it lies.
– Bobby Jones

I like to look on the good side of things.
What were the good things of the day or
good things that happened to me?
– Roy Vomastek

1

Prologue: The Lucky Ball

On a beautiful summer afternoon, 78-year-old Dr. Roy Vomastek walked slowly through the high fescue grass bordering the 17th green of Dr. Alister MacKenzie's magnificent Crystal Downs Country Club, desperately searching for his golf ball.

Roy's teenaged caddie and several members from the gallery joined quietly in the search. For the past few days, Roy had turned back the clock on Father Time. He'd held his own against the best golfers in the club, men 20-to-40 years younger. He was so close to pulling off the unthinkable.

Roy trudged through the rough, exhausted from playing six rounds in three days, hoping to find a flash of white hidden in the thick, tangled grass. Hoping for one more miracle.

But it wasn't to be.

His time up, Roy conceded the hole to his opponent and

headed towards the 18th tee. There was one hole left to play in the 2010 Crystal Downs Country Club Championship.

And Roy had lost his lucky ball.

ESCANABA
MICHIGAN

CRYSTAL
DOWNS

1932

AUGUSTA
GEORGIA

2

Augusta, Crystal Downs & Escanaba

January 1932

In the midst of the Great Depression, legendary amateur golf champion Robert Tyre "Bobby" Jones, Jr. was overseeing the construction of Augusta National Golf Club in Augusta, Georgia with the help of Clifford Roberts. Jones, only 29 years old, was little more than a year removed from his magical summer of 1930 when he had captured "The Grand Slam" by winning the British Amateur, British Open, United States Open and United States Amateur Championships. Jones had designed his new course with Dr. Alister MacKenzie and his vision was a year away from its January 1933 opening and two years away from hosting its first Invitational Tournament that would eventually be known as The Masters.

Meanwhile, 1000 miles northwest of Augusta, near the quiet little town of Frankfort, Michigan, Walkley Bailey Ewing had pressed on in the face of the Great Depression in pursuit of his own dream to build a special course. The second nine holes of Crystal Downs Country Club had been completed and would open for play later that spring. Four years earlier, in 1928, after Dr. Alister MacKenzie had finished his work at Cypress Point and was en route across the United States to catch a boat back to England, Ewing had convinced him to detour up to Northern Michigan. Enthralled by the site, MacKenzie designed a masterpiece and left it in the hands of his American associate, Perry Maxwell, to oversee construction.

While Jones was crafting his masterpiece and Ewing's dream was under snow, 120 miles northwest of Frankfort, across Lake Michigan, in the small town of Escanaba on the shores of Michigan's upper peninsula, Della and Charles Vomastek welcomed their fourth child, Roy, into the world on January 17, 1932.

But no one in the Vomastek household was thinking about golf. Roy's father, Charles, had suffered a severe head injury while serving in combat in World War I and was haunted with complications that had required several surgeries. While battling his poor health, Charles worked as a press operator for the Escanaba Daily news and was constantly looking for new opportunities to provide for his family. He became an expert on printing presses and developed a side business, traveling the towns of Michigan's upper peninsula servicing and repairing presses.

When Roy was only a few months old, his father fell ill again and was transported to Chicago for yet another operation. Charles' surgeon was the renowned Loyal Davis—First Lady Nancy Reagan's stepfather who later became her adoptive father. Despite having one of the top neurosurgeons in the world, Roy's father didn't make it.

The next several years were extraordinarily difficult for Roy's widowed mother as she struggled to provide for her four young children. She worked in a local hardware store and received welfare funds from the government's Emergency Relief Act but was unable to earn enough to provide for the family of five. With no other options for income in the face of the Great Depression, Della was forced to send Roy's oldest brother, Bob, and sister, Mary Ann, to live with relatives in Wisconsin. Having already lost her husband and now letting go of her two oldest children so that she might provide for her two youngest, Della was heartbroken and vowed to find a way to earn enough to provide for Roy and his older brother, Charles, until she could reunite her family.

In 1939, when Roy was seven years old, World War II broke out. After the USA entered the war following the Japanese attack on Pearl Harbor in 1941, much of American industry was mobilized to support the war effort. By 1942, Detroit, Michigan had become a hot bed for jobs so Della packed their few belongings and bought three one-way bus tickets for herself, Roy, now 10, and Charles, hoping to build a better life and finally reunite her family. She found a job as a civilian secretary for the U.S. Naval Ordinance Department and a home for herself and her two boys in a small upstairs flat in a tough Detroit neighborhood near 6th and Brush.

It had been seven long and painful years but she had persevered. Roy's mother sent word to her relatives that Bob and Mary Ann could finally return. Roy's sister rejoined the family but his brother refused—Bob had built a new life and didn't want to return. Della was devastated but determined to make the best of it. For the first time in the decade since she'd lost her husband, Della felt she could build a happier life for her family.

And her youngest child, Roy, was ready to pitch in.

"We all kind of stuck together and helped each other," Roy

recalled. "And we just worked. In those days, your milk was delivered by a horse-drawn truck. I started working for this guy—they called me a jumper and I'd jump off the truck while it was still moving. I'd run and take the milk up to the houses and bring the old bottles back. A lot of people would leave a list—I want cottage cheese or cream—and you'd carry all that with you. So I did that during The War. And I also had a newspaper route. It was work, work, work. But if you wanted something, if you didn't work, you didn't get it."

Roy's appreciation for work and sense of initiative would come to define his life and in the summer of 1942, introduced him to a game that changed his life...

A kid grows up a lot faster on the golf course. Golf teaches you how to behave.
– Jack Nicklaus

3

The Caddie

Summer 1942

The early-to-mid 1940s was a transition period in American golf. Following the amateur successes of Francis Ouimet and Bobby Jones, Walter Hagen had blazed a trail in the 1920s and '30s for his fellow professionals, becoming the first superstar professional golfer and one of the most famous athletes of his era alongside baseball's Babe Ruth and boxing's Jack Dempsey. Byron Nelson, Ben Hogan and Sam Snead, all born in 1912, had followed Hagen's trail and taken golf further.

Roy heard from some of the older kids in the neighborhood that he could make fifty cents per round as a caddie carrying clubs at Palmer Park Golf Course—a place renowned for money games, drawing a number of Detroit's best golfers including D.B.R Brown, Midge Cova and even world heavyweight champion boxer Joe Louis.

Without a father at home, Roy gravitated towards the men around the golf course. Like so many other boys before and after him, golf provided Roy a glimpse behind the curtain of male camaraderie and adulthood, offering invaluable insights into life, family, business and the workings of the world.

The players took an instant liking to the happy, eager little kid and showed Roy the ropes for being a good caddie. Roy was soon guaranteed a loop whenever he showed up. Midge Cova, in particular, took Roy under his wing, believing he brought him good luck. When Midge travelled to other courses to play a match or tournament, he would drive by the Vomasteks' flat and pick Roy up to caddie for him. One day, Midge gave Roy a couple of clubs and taught him how to swing. Young Roy was hooked and began hitting balls every chance he could find.

"I started off with one club, a 5-iron. Then I had three clubs. Older golfers would give me a club once in awhile. I never had a full set of clubs until after I got out of the army. Even when I played golf for four years in high school, I never had a full set of clubs. I just had a make-up set, an old beat-up this-and-that."

Little did young Roy know the role those clubs and game would play in his life.

4

———

Reporting For Duty

Summer 1949

GOLF TEAM
Bottom Row: Tom Richardson, Roy Vomastek (Captain), Joe Schultz.
Second Row: Constantine Margaritis, Jim Gidley.

The Cass Tech High School Golf Team

Roy had the good fortune of attending Cass Tech High School, the best academic public school in Detroit, thanks to Roy's best friend, a basketball player who had encouraged Roy to join him there. It was six miles from home and Della gave Roy bus fare each day because she believed in the value of a strong education. Unbeknownst to her, Roy kept the money, walked three miles to the busy intersection of 3rd and 6th and hitchhiked the rest of the way. Roy loved attending Cass Tech, was an excellent student and became captain of the golf team.

After graduating from high school in the summer of 1949, however, he was at a loss of what to do. With no money for college and no angles on a scholarship, Roy faced the prospect of finding a job and staying in Detroit. But what he really wanted to do was see the world. A few days after graduating, Roy visited the local Army recruiting office. He tested high, was offered an opportunity to train as a medical technician and enlisted immediately

"Someone said if you get in the army, don't volunteer for anything. Well, I'm just a 17-year-old kid, I don't know any different. I'd been at basic training at Fort Riley in Kansas for about two weeks. Every morning you had to stand at formation and they'd count heads. And one day the First Sergeant, who's the boss, says, 'Can anybody type?' And I raised my hand and said I could. I really couldn't. But I figured I could figure it out. And he said, 'Come on, get out of the formation, you're done with this.' The company clerk, who had to type out the morning report of the company, had to go on sick leave and he was going to be gone for the next four weeks. So they made me the company clerk. I didn't have to stand in any formations. I didn't have to get up at like six in the morning or stand in line to eat. And the best thing was, when we had to do our rifle training, everyone had to march with a backpack and their rifle about 15 miles

up and back to the rifle range. I got to drive in a jeep. And I played ping pong. I could type out the report in about an hour and I played ping pong with the company commander every day, because he liked to play ping pong. And that's my life. It's just a miracle. I call it a miracle. It's something that's just so dumb. Wasn't planned, nothing's planned. But it just happens. Things just work out for me."

After completing basic training, Roy was sent to Brook Army Medical Center at Fort Sam Houston in San Antonio. He thrived and after finishing his medical tech training was asked where he would like to be assigned. Without hesitation, Roy said overseas. He was offered duty in Japan or Germany and having always been fascinated by Japan, jumped at that opportunity. Roy was told to report to Seattle for departure after his 60-day leave but surprised his commanding officers by saying he didn't want a leave, he wanted to go immediately. Struck by the unusual request, they agreed and Roy was off to Seattle to board the Naval transport ship to Japan. Roy didn't know it yet, but his eagerness to leave immediately possibly saved his life.

When Roy got on the ship to Japan, his initiative again improved his situation.

"I was down at F deck which is way down at the bottom of the boat. There's no air conditioning. You had a hammock to sleep in and you had to stand in these long lines for every meal. So they announce over the speaker system the first day I was on there, 'Any lab technicians interested in working?' I volunteered and went up there. They said you're just what we need. They needed a lab tech because they didn't have one to run the lab. So they moved me up on C deck. I had an innerspring mattress. I never had to stand in line for chow. I got to eat with the Navy guys. It was just a miracle."

Two months after Roy arrived in Japan, a number of his

classmates from training who had also selected duty in Japan headed across the Pacific following their 60-day leave. En route, the Korean War broke out and their ship was redirected. His former classmates, trained as lab technicians, were given rifles and sent to the front lines. Many died or were badly wounded and the casualties were transported to the medical facility in Japan where Roy was stationed which became an evacuation hospital for the Korean War. Roy's bedroom in the hospital was needed for overflow so he and others ended up living in tents out on the baseball diamond. As he watched the bodies of his classmates coming through, Roy pondered what it all meant.

"I wasn't thinking that a war was going to start when I left early, I just wanted to go see the world. I'm seeing them come in...oh my God."

For the rest of his life, Roy would always remember the impact of his simple act of taking initiative.

Roy's brush with fate drove him to appreciate each day even more. He quickly adjusted to life in Japan and developed a deep love for the people, the culture and the land. His jovial personality created a wide network of friends. Being a gifted natural athlete, he won bowling tournaments, ping pong tournaments and even became involved in the new sport of track bicycle racing called Keirin which had originated only a few years earlier in 1948. Roy became close friends through Keirin with a very talented young racer, Katsuaki Matsumoto.

Matsumoto was far better than Roy and had the potential to compete at the highest levels. Roy had recently heard of a new development back in the USA—metal rims for racing bicycles—so he wrote his sister, Mary Ann, asking her to send him a pair, believing they would give him an advantage over the bamboo wheel rims that often shattered and added an unwelcomed element of danger to the sport. When the metal wheels arrived, his hunch was quickly confirmed. Roy was amazed by their strength as well as their light weight compared to the bamboo rims. He could surely win many races with them. So he decided not to use them.

Instead, Roy presented them as a gift to Matsumoto who installed them on his bike, went on a winning streak and soon captured the national championship. Returning the gift of friendship, Matsumoto presented Roy with his national championship trophy. Matsumoto went on to become the Babe Ruth of his sport, the winningest racer in Keirin history and won the highest honor in Japanese sports, the Japan Professional Sports Grand Prize in 1972. (Other winners have included baseball greats Sadaharu Oh, Hideo Nomo, Ichiro Suzuki, Hideki Matsui and golfers Masashi "Jumbo" Ozaki and two-time winner Ryo Ishikawa, the teenage phenom who made headlines for announcing he would donate his entire on-course winnings in 2011 to victims of the Japanese earthquake and tsunami.)

Matsumoto retired from Keirin in 1981 with 1341 wins, a record that still stands.

Roy and Katsuaki Matsumoto

Roy's knack for improving the lives of those around him paid off for his fellow servicemen as well. The enterprising Roy, always looking for opportunities and always willing to work, accepted the task of managing the NCO (Non-Commissioned Officers) club in addition to his normal duties as a medical technician. It was a sleepy little club that offered poor food and little else. Any profit was sent to the main NCO club in Tokyo. Due to their proximity to Korea, soldiers engaged in combat would often come to the base on weekend passes and frequent the club. Roy was struck by the idea that a vibrant club would be a real service and outlet for the war-weary soldiers but couldn't get any funds committed for it. One day, the obvious answer struck him. If he were to begin making "repairs" to the club in the form of improvements to the building and service, there might not be any profits to send back to Tokyo. Roy got to work. Within a year he had transformed the club into a destination with fine dining, slot machines, orchestras and dancing.

Roy's remarkable entrepreneurism within the typically regimented military structure gave him influence beyond his rank.

"A company has a commanding officer and the First Sergeant. The commanding officer gets the directives from headquarters and tells the First Sergeant what to do but the First Sergeant runs the show. He's the boss. He controls everything. And the company commander, he just signs orders. After about two years in the Army, while I'm over at the hospital, I got well connected because I ran the NCO club. I was kind of the power broker and I could do tremendous favors for people...such as get them liquor real cheap and good food real cheap. And do a lot of other favors. Plus, I was head of the medical lab and gonorrhea was rampant. No one wanted to have that on their record, so guys would come to me and I would check them out and if that's what they had, I could get them the penicillin and get it so they were taken care of and it never showed on their record. So it was like a poker game. And eventually, I accumulated a lot of chips or a lot of favors. But I just did it because it was the right thing to do.

So the Korean War wasn't going well and my brother who was a year-and-a-half older than me gets drafted. They sent him to Colorado and taught him to be a tank driver. And my mother wrote me a letter. Told me my brother was going to Korea as a tank driver. Well, I thought, that doesn't sound too good. So I told her, 'You be sure to tell him anybody who went to Korea at this time, they took the boat over and landed in Yokohama.' That was the distribution center. Then everyone was sent from

Yokohama to wherever they were assigned. I went to my friend, the First Sergeant, and told him my brother was coming over to be a tank driver. We got a guy here in our hospital unit that wants to go to Korea in the worst way. He wants to be a hero and all this stuff, wants to be fighting. He's frustrated with not being on the front lines. So we created a swap. I went to the civilian guy who was in charge of the lab with me and I told him about this and he said, 'If you can teach your brother lab stuff, I have no problems with that.' So my brother, when he lands in Yokohama, calls me and I said, 'OK, just sit tight for a day or two and your new orders are coming down and you're going to be shipped up to this hospital rather than going to Korea and the guy in our unit's going to take your place and he's going to go to Korea.' So sure enough, that's what happened. My brother ended up at our hospital and I taught him how to do lab work and he ended up being the lab technician on night call and didn't have to go to Korea as a tank driver."

Matsumoto and Roy's brother had discovered first hand something that people would discover for the next 60 years—the benefit of being in Roy's orbit. It didn't only tend to make your days happier and more interesting, it could also save your life.

During this time, a young Japanese nurse also recognized the special spark in Roy and the two fell in love. With the end of his duty nearing, Roy came up with an idea. He would seek permission to stay and become the full-time manager of the NCO club. It didn't take long for the idea to gain steam and for everyone to agree since the club was a huge hit. Almost everything was in place. There was one more thing Roy really wanted and that was to get married. He proposed and she accepted. Roy excitedly wrote his mother to share the great news.

About two weeks later, Roy was called into the base

commander's office. As soon as he walked into the room, Roy knew something was wrong. He was perplexed to see an MP officer standing guard as the base commander looked at Roy sternly, "I don't know who the hell you pissed off, but I've got orders from the Secretary of the Army to send you home right now!"

Unbeknownst to Roy, Roy's mother was furious when she learned her son wanted to marry a Japanese girl. Della still considered the Japanese enemies as a result of World War II. Upon receiving Roy's letter informing her of his engagement, she had immediately contacted Roy's oldest brother, Bob, who was then living in Texas and was friends with a powerful politician who had a direct connection to the Secretary of the Army.

Standing in the base commander's office in Japan, Roy's mind was spinning as the MP stepped forward, put Roy in handcuffs and led him out of the office.

Within hours, Roy was on a ship back to the states. Because his brother's time was almost up, they sent him home with Roy, too. Roy wasn't allowed to speak to anyone and wasn't allowed to say goodbyes.

Bewildered, Roy still had the presence of mind to request to go straight to the hospital on the troop ship when he boarded.

"I said, 'I'm a lab tech, do you need any help?' And they said, 'Oh yeah, get your stuff from down below and come on up here.'"

Roy had enlisted to see the world and his eagerness to start his adventure without delay had possibly saved his life. He'd crossed an ocean, turned a sleepy NCO club into a hot spot, played a small part in the creation of an eventual Japanese sports legend, fallen in love and gotten engaged. But the universe had other plans for him and had summoned him back to his roots in Michigan.

He would never see or speak to his fiancée again.

5

─────────

Building A New Life

1952–1956

When Roy returned home from Japan he was confronted by his livid mother. The lingering effects of World War I had claimed his father's life and now lingering animosity from World War II had reached into the Korean War and stolen his first love. Roy was heartbroken but realized there was no point in arguing. He would not be allowed to return to Japan with the military and if he attempted to do so on his own, it would emotionally destroy his mother. The adventure was over.

One day, a letter arrived from his former fiancée—she had met another man and was getting married. It was the final communication between them. The next couple of years were painful for Roy as he struggled to figure out where he fit while trying to let go of the love and dreams he had been forced to leave behind against his will.

But Roy did what he always did. Made the best of things,

worked hard and began looking for his next miracle. After working in a hospital for about a year for little pay and with the auto industry at full steam, Della was able to get Roy a job at the General Motors HydraMatic plant down the road from her house where she also worked. While it wasn't work that inspired him, there was a silver lining—Roy worked the afternoon shift, leaving the mornings free to play golf.

Roy hadn't played much since high school but it wasn't long before he was hooked again. He began frequenting Hawthorne Valley where the jockeys and horse trainers from the Detroit Race Course in Livonia played money games. Roy wasn't a gambler but the guys loved him and always invited him to play in the matches.

Golf was in the midst of the post-war boom lead by Byron Nelson, Ben Hogan and Sam Snead. Like almost any golfer who's had a bit of game, Roy flirted with the idea of playing professionally.

"When I was working for General Motors and playing a lot of golf, I thought a dream would have been to be a professional golfer. But I played with some good players and realized I could never be that good. So after that I never thought about it ever. It was just fun. I just had such a love of playing, you don't know who's going to show up that day to play...looking forward to beautiful shots..."

Having decided golf would remain a hobby, Roy's willingness to work various jobs to earn his living led to a chance encounter that would define the rest of his life.

"I was working for General Motors and on weekends I'd once in a while cut meat at a butcher shop in a small supermarket. One day, I went in to do some shopping and came around the corner with my cart and almost ran right into this pretty cashier. I tried to avoid her and I knocked over this big thing of canned

corn. I'll never forget it—it was all stacked up and I just blasted it. So that's how I met Shirley. To apologize, I took her to a movie. We lived in Redford Township which was a suburb of Detroit and turned out she lived about four blocks from me."

The movie was the 1954 theatrical re-release of *Gone With the Wind*, reformatted to the wide screen. When Roy arrived to pick up Shirley for the movie, there was a surprise addition—Shirley's mother was joining them.

Roy and Shirley started dating soon after and were married in 1955. Their son, Andrew, was born within a year and the responsibilities of work and family left little time for golf.

Like many husbands and fathers before and after him, Roy understood the need to set the game aside to focus on life and handle his obligations. He made a deal with Shirley to stop playing and put his golf clubs in the closet where they would remain for years.

First comes my wife and my children.
Next comes my profession, the law.
Finally, and never a life in itself, comes
golf.
– Bobby Jones

6

Husband, Father & Provider

1956–1962

Roy found his job at General Motors far from ideal. He believed in working hard and giving his best effort. At the time, the United Auto Workers Local was involved in a power struggle with management over work rules and production quotas. A union official pulled Roy aside one day and told him he was working too quickly and it was causing problems for the other workers. There was an unspoken understanding about the level of effort workers should give and Roy needed to adhere to it. This went against everything Roy stood for in his core, everything he'd learned as a young kid hustling and working, then serving in the Army. Roy knew at that moment it was no longer the job for him and quit.

He set out to find a job using the medical technician skills he had learned in the Army. Roy responded to a newspaper ad for a job with a local doctor, Dr. Chase Edward Matthews, and was hired as his X-ray technician. Roy was grateful for the work although the schedule was much more demanding than his job at the auto plant. Roy worked three shifts daily from 9am-to-noon, 1-to-5pm and 6-to-9pm, then often tacked on additional night work with other odd jobs.

After the birth of their second child, Edward Chase (named after Roy's new boss), in 1957, Roy and Shirley decided to purchase a small home. The pressure was on the 25-year-old Roy to make more money to support his growing family and he began to feel a building restlessness in the grind of his work, a feeling that he was capable of more. After talking with Shirley, Roy decided to enroll in a night class at the University of Detroit to see if he was capable of college-level studies. He figured if he could get through college and earn a degree, he could become a teacher and build a better life for his family.

Roy loved chemistry in high school so he started with an evening chemistry class at the university. As fate would have it, Roy's lab partner, Mike Wellman, played on the University of Detroit golf team and one evening in class asked Roy if he played golf. Roy said he did but that it had been a few years since he had touched a club. Mike told him about an annual intramural golf tournament that some players from the team played in and encouraged Roy to come out and play for the fun of it.

Roy dusted off his clubs and practiced for about a week, finding a half-hour here and there between work shifts to work off the rust. He liked the way he was hitting the ball so he signed up for the tournament...

And won.

Mike was flabbergasted and suggested Roy try out for the golf team. Not only was he sure Roy would make the team, he'd probably get a scholarship. Roy was thrilled. A scholarship would mean he could afford to go to school full-time and get a degree—all while playing golf! Mike told his coach about Roy, arranged the tryout and sure enough, Roy easily made the team and was awarded a full scholarship.

Roy told Dr. Matthews about his good fortune and that he was leaving his job to enroll in college and pursue a chemistry degree with the goal of becoming a teacher. While the scholarship meant Roy didn't have to keep a full-time job, money was still tight. In order to cut costs, Roy and Shirley sold their small home and moved their family in with Roy's mother. To further help ends meet, Roy found a night job at an industrial medical clinic that gave him a little income while still leaving time to study.

The next four years were a juggle of family, studying, work and college golf with Roy eventually being named captain of the team. While Roy was in his last year at the University of Detroit, he received a phone call out of the blue from his former boss, Dr. Matthews, inviting him and Shirley to a University of Michigan football game. Over dinner following the game, Dr. Matthews asked Roy about his plans after graduation. When Roy described his plan to teach high school, Dr. Matthews asked why he wasn't considering attending medical school.

The thought had never entered Roy's mind. He had a family to support and couldn't afford it. Dr. Matthews saw it differently and presented a life-changing offer. If Roy could get admitted to a medical school, Dr. Matthews would pay his tuition and expenses. In exchange, Roy would promise to return to Michigan after med school and buy out his practice, allowing Dr. Matthews to retire.

Roy was almost 30 and hadn't planned on attending more school but recognized a miracle when he saw one. After years of toiling away as a medical lab technician working for doctors, he could become a doctor himself!

7

The Med Student

1963–1967

Roy began applying to med schools and was admitted to Kirksville College of Osteopathic Medicine near St. Louis, Missouri in the fall of 1963 at 31 years old. As Roy loaded up his young family and their few possessions to make the drive from Michigan, he couldn't help but think back to the similar journey in search of a better life he had made 21 years earlier with his mom and brother.

The Vomasteks moved into married housing and Roy began his studies. Golf had paid for college which led to med school but once again, Roy put away the clubs. He was extremely grateful for the opportunity to be at Kirksville on behalf of Dr. Matthews and knew he had to focus on his studies and his family. Roy was a straight-A student his first semester and everything was going according to plan until a shocking letter arrived from Mrs. Mathews one day.

Dr. Matthews had died suddenly.

There was no more money to pay for Roy's education. Mrs. Matthews was selling her late husband's practice and regrettably could not afford to help Roy any longer.

Roy was devastated as the reality of his situation came crashing down. He told Shirley he had to drop out. The only option was to return to Michigan and pursue his original plan to be a chemistry teacher. And he'd do what he always did. Work hard and look for the next miracle.

The next day, Roy met with Dean Walters who listened intently as Roy told him about the death of his benefactor, Dr. Matthews, and his plan to return to Michigan. After a long pause, Dean Walters told Roy to go back to class. The faculty was extremely impressed with Roy and would hate to see him go. He asked Roy to give him a couple of weeks to try to figure something out. No promises, but he'd see what could be done.

Two weeks later, Dean Walters called Roy back into his office. He had a possible solution if Roy was interested. It had never been done before—the staff and the board had agreed to fund Roy's tuition if he alternated six months of class work with six months as a full-time teachers' assistant. It would take Roy an extra year to complete his studies but at least he could stay in school, with one additional catch—there was no assistance available for housing. Roy, Shirley and their boys would have to move out of the married housing complex.

Roy was thrilled, his dream was still alive. He set out to find the least expensive housing they could make work which turned out to be a small log cabin for rent in the countryside near Kirksville. It didn't have central heat but it did have running water and at $50 a month, fit their meager budget. The Vomasteks moved in and made the most of it. They planted a garden and Roy raised and sold beagles. He also hunted for food on the weekends, mostly rabbit. Despite the hardship, they grew to enjoy country life.

Andrew, Ed, Roy & Shirley Vomastek in front of their log cabin in Missouri

"The kids wanted a pony, so I bought this pony at auction. I might have paid twenty dollars for it. Then they wanted to go ride out in the woods or around and they didn't have anyone to go with. I decided I better get an adult horse so I could ride with them. Then this guy I knew had a stallion and we bred both of them. So then we went from 2 horses to 4 horses. And then I found an old buggy at an auction and this horse that I had was broke to pull a buggy...so we'd pull a buggy around and sometimes go to town in the buggy."

While Roy was raising beagles, hunting rabbits, breeding ponies and occasionally pulling a buggy, he kept thriving as a student and graduated from medical school in 1967 at the age of 35.

8

The Medical Intern

1967–1968

Roy and Shirley had always intended to return to Michigan to raise their family and they settled on The Saginaw Osteopathic Hospital in Saginaw, Michigan about 110 miles from Detroit for Roy's internship.

"There were about 35 interns. Since I was the old guy, because I started med school late, they just said we're going to make you in charge of the interns. I had to form schedules and go to certain staff functions and I'd get the news and scuttlebutt and pass it on to the interns."

One of the other things this entailed was coordinating interviews for the interns with prospective employers. Ed Meyering was the mayor of McBain, a tiny rural northern Michigan town in Missaukee County. McBain began as a settlement around a sawmill founded by the McBain brothers in 1887, got a train station and post office in 1888, incorporated as a village in 1893 and as a city in 1907. The farming town of about 400 residents had been without a physician for eight years and the good mayor felt it was his personal responsibility to the citizens to find one.

"They were dying to get a doctor in this small town and no one would go. So the mayor would come to the hospital in Saginaw and say, 'We're looking for someone, come up and visit.' I met with this guy a couple times and I'd pass on the word to the other interns. I was planning on going to a big town, Battle Creek, because I had a friend who was a doctor there and I was going to join him. But I kept going back to the interns and saying, 'Guys, this town really needs a doctor. Someone oughta look at it.' And no one would."

As Roy neared the end of his internship, he began his interview process. He felt bad for Mayor Meyering and suggested to Shirley they pay McBain a courtesy visit. They'd take Andy and Ed and make it a family outing, just a nice drive on a day off. Roy called the Mayor who was thrilled.

As the Vomasteks drove into McBain for the first time a few weeks later, a marching band proceeded down the street. They were confused—it wasn't a holiday. When they saw Mayor Meyering and a large group waving and holding up signs welcoming them to the town, it hit them. The parade was in their honor!

The Mayor wasn't leaving anything to chance. His town needed a doctor and Roy was his best shot. Over a community potluck dinner in the little high school gym, home of the McBain Rural Agricultural School Ramblers, the Mayor presented their offer. A house and office rent-free for the year and a $25,000 interest-free loan to buy equipment and get started.

The Vomasteks were overwhelmed and promised the Mayor they'd consider his offer.

"When we were driving back to Saginaw, we got to talking about it. And we said, 'Well, let's try it. What the heck. We got nothing to lose. We'll try it for a year and if it doesn't really work out, or we don't like it, we can always go to the big city since we were kind of big city people from growing up in Detroit.'"

Roy called the Mayor a few days later to accept.

McBain thought it was hiring a doctor who had spent time in the Army as a lab technician. They didn't realize they were also getting the guy who had turned a sleepy NCO club into the hottest night club around.

The Vomasteks were moving to McBain and McBain would never be the same again.

9

McBain & The Vomasteks

The McBain Presbyterian Church and parsonage

When Roy, Shirley, 13-year-old Andy and 10-year-old Ed

moved into the McBain Presbyterian Church's parsonage in the summer of 1968, the high school didn't have a football team because it conflicted with the fall harvest. No dances meant no prom. And no TV antennas in the town, at least none at first glance. Those that had them kept them in their attic so they could get reception without the tell-tale antenna up on the roof because they weren't supposed to be watching TV much and certainly never on Sundays.

"One of the first things I did was put a TV antenna out on the roof because I wanted a better reception so I could watch football games on Sunday. That kind of broke the barrier. And I guess someone said, 'Well the doctor has one, it must be okay.' And pretty soon it was OK. Everyone had TV antennas."

Before Roy was through, the town had football, dancing and prom, too.

Dr. Roy Vomastek opened the doors of his practice in July of 1968 and hired a young girl, Marlene, right out of high school to be his assistant.

The Vomasteks quickly acclimated and fell in love with McBain but living in town presented one challenge. Because the town had extended such a generous offer to help them get started and been without a doctor for some time, there weren't any boundaries.

"Say they had a sick child. All day long I'm in the office, they wouldn't bring the child in. But 8, 9, 10 o'clock at night, they're knocking on the door, saying, 'My baby's sick what are you going to do about it?' So we decided to move out of town and tried to find a place. But since it was an agricultural area, none of the farmers wanted to sell their land. We found a piece of wilderness land that wasn't being farmed, about 280 acres. The guy who owned it was Mr. Dexter and I'd never met him since he lived downstate. I wrote him a letter and asked if he'd

sell me 10 acres. He responded he'd sell me the whole thing for an incredible deal. It was $1000 down and the payments were like $100 a month and the interest was maybe 3%. So we bought it and we built a house. I built a lake on it. Dammed up a stream. And we had a fish pond in the back. Just fantastic hunting. I fell in love with country living. But we had all this land and didn't know what to do with it."

And the always-enterprising Roy wasn't going to let 280 acres just *sit there*. He started buying beef cattle and raising them. The market was decent and he began making some money to supplement his medical practice. During this time, the doctor in Marion, the next town over, quit and his patients started making the drive to McBain. But due to the gas shortages of the time, Roy didn't see the sense in all the sick people driving to see him.

"I said it's easier for me to move there in the afternoon rather than have all these people driving."

So Roy added a second office. On days he didn't have a surgery scheduled, Roy spent his mornings in McBain and his afternoons in Marion before stopping by the hospital. For a long time, Roy was the only doctor in all of Missaukee County.

Meanwhile, back on the farm, Roy was up to about 300 head of cattle. They added some buildings and Shirley, four months pregnant, planted trees surrounding the driveway and home. Then the beef market went south.

"Michigan State University said you have to go dairy. The price of milk was $16 for a hundred pounds which was big money. And it was all subsidized by the government, a win-win situation. So I borrowed way more money than I should have. And of course, in those days the banks would let you have all the money you wanted. So we switched over to dairy. We had two little kids. And we put them to work on the farm. It was a big dairy operation."

Roy the doctor had gone from cattle farmer to dairy farmer. By 1971, Roy and Shirley had added two more children to their family, Dan and Rebecca. When Roy wasn't busy seeing patients and managing the farm, he added more hobbies along the way. Roy earned a pilot's license and developed a passion for flying, bought a boat to go cruising on Lake Michigan and embraced the 1970s with gusto, sporting a perm and chauffeuring Shirley in his new Porsche on nights out for dancing.

Earlier in the 1970s, a group of local guys decided it was time for the county to have a golf course. The closest course at the time was in Cadillac and thanks to the rise of golf on television and the popularity of Arnold Palmer and Jack Nicklaus, local kids were getting the bug and wanted to play golf. Roy still wasn't playing—his family, practice and farm left no time—but he agreed to help. A couple of guys from Lake City and McBain found an old hay field and sold shares in the club for $50 to raise money. Roy lent some of his farm equipment and a local farmer who knew a few things about growing grass became the superintendent. They smoothed out the land, pushed up the greens with a bulldozer and enlisted kids and friends to help pick all the stones off the fairways before they planted. Soon, the Missaukee Golf Club opened for play.

Roy's son, Ed, was about 16 at the time and a gifted high school athlete. He started going out to the club to play with his friends the summer of his junior year and picked the game up quickly. He also began bugging his dad to play. When Roy declined, the bugging turned to taunting and then flat-out challenging his old man that he could beat him.

"He got to pushing me...and so I started playing again. We were very competitive once he got me going."

Once again, Roy's initiative had unintended positive consequences. Helping build a golf club to give back to his community led his son to pull Roy back into the game. Roy and Ed would later meet a couple of times in the finals of the Missaukee Club Championship with each winning once.

A few years later, Roy got another call out of the blue that would change his life. His good friend, Dr. Jim Johnson, a fine amateur player, invited Roy to come play Crystal Downs Country Club, another golf course that a doctor who had served in the military had a hand in creating, 70 miles northwest of Missaukee Golf Club.

Simply put, if you haven't seen Crystal Downs, your education in golf course architecture is incomplete.
— Tom Doak
Golf Course Architect

It was designed by the greatest golf course architect that ever lived when he was at the peak of his design creativity and built on just an incredible piece of property. It's an amazing collection of holes without an average hole on the course.
— Fred Muller
Head Professional
Crystal Downs Country Club

10

———

Crystal Downs Country Club

Mother Nature creates the great courses, architects shape them and players christen them but the great courses become even greater from what transpires on them. The shots made, rounds played, friendships created and tournaments contested.

Walkley Ewing's dream to build a course for families and friends to spend their summers together where memories could be made, traditions created and the torch passed from generation to generation officially became a reality with an opening party on July 4, 1929. The name Crystal Downs was bestowed by Benjamin P. Merrick, a Grand Rapids attorney who, like Dr. Alister MacKenzie, found it reminded him of terrain in England known as "downs land." The beautiful English-style clubhouse designed by Alexander McColl remains unchanged today, standing on one of the highest points of the property overlooking Lake Michigan, Sleeping Bear Dunes, Crystal Lake and the golf course.

Regarded as one of the top courses in America, a timelessness permeates the club, its heritage carefully guarded by the members who value the course's uniqueness and transcendent beauty. Like all great courses, Crystal Downs has an aura, a result of the harmony of land and design, a magic that comes up through your feet, in through your eyes and overwhelms your senses.

Walkley Bailey Ewing was born in 1901 in Grand Haven, Michigan and was 25 years old when he discovered the narrow strip of land between Crystal Lake and Lake Michigan while hiking along the east coast of Lake Michigan. He bought the options for the special setting and knew he needed to find the right architect. Ewing wrote to Robert Hunter, who had written a book on golf course architecture, seeking advice. Hunter had recently worked with Dr. Alister MacKenzie in California and highly recommended him.

Dr. Alister MacKenzie was born in England in 1870. After serving as an Army surgeon during the Boer War in South Africa, he was working in private practice when renowned architect Harry Colt came to Leeds to redesign MacKenzie's home course, The Alwoodly Club. MacKenzie's interaction with Colt lead him to start designing courses on the side. His desire to go into the profession full-time was interrupted by World War I when he reenlisted in the British Army and ended up creating breakthrough camouflage theories and tactics that he'd later utilize in his golf course designs.

Following The Great War, MacKenzie committed himself to designing courses for a living which lead to a consulting project to chart and map The Old Course at St. Andrew's. Like Dr. Roy Vomastek, Dr. Alister MacKenzie wanted to see the world and in 1926 he set off for America in the hopes of leaving his mark by creating classic courses.

When Ewing went searching for his architect, MacKenzie had recently finished his work on Cypress Point Club in California and was preparing to head East across the United States to catch a ship back home to England. It was still a couple of years before MacKenzie's work on Cypress Point would inspire Bobby Jones to enlist him to help design his dream course down in Georgia.

MacKenzie had another gem to create first.

Ewing located MacKenzie and was able to convince him to come up to Northern Michigan for a visit. MacKenzie met up with his co-designer, Perry Maxwell, a renowned architect in the lower Midwest who was still several years away from designing his own masterpiece, Prairie Dunes, in Hutchinson, Kansas. MacKenzie was instantly smitten with Ewing's land, laid out a design, then left construction in Maxwell's hands and returned to England. The first nine holes of Crystal Downs Country Club opened for play in 1929. Undaunted by the stock market crash that fall, Ewing pressed forward with the second nine by raising money from prospective members. The entire course opened for play in 1932, the same year Roy was born.

When Roy took Dr. Jim Johnson up on his invitation to play it for the first time, Crystal Downs was still relatively unknown in golfing circles. Tucked up in seclusion in Northern Michigan, away from a major population center and far from both coasts, the club and its members had chosen to stay out of the limelight. In addition, the attention in the 1970s was focused on the modern designers as opposed to the classic and minimalist work of the old masters such as MacKenzie, Donald Ross, A.W. Tillinghast, Seth Raynor, and C.B. MacDonald.

Roy instantly fell in love with the beautiful course—it was unlike any he had ever seen, demanding all sorts of shots with different lies, wind and the most challenging greens he had every played.

Tom Doak captures its essence well in his book, *The Confidential Guide to Golf Courses.*

"Four factors conspire to defeat you: The wind which can blow equally hard from north or south at any time of the year. The greens—some of the fiercest ever contoured by the team of MacKenzie and Maxwell. The thick native roughs, which add so much to the character of the landscape, but threaten to turn any wild drive into a double bogey. MacKenzie's penchant for designing holes on the borderline of par, where strokes can slip away so easily or be regained so dramatically."

After their round, Jim suggested to Roy that he join Crystal Downs and offered to be his sponsor. Roy was enchanted by the course but reluctantly declined, citing his obligations to work and family. There just wasn't enough time.

Jim told Roy it was a standing offer he could take him up on anytime and Roy left that day enamored by Crystal Downs, hoping he'd get to play it again.

11

The Golfer Returns

Roy continued working and focusing on family with his and Shirley's efforts paying off as their three sons and daughter all graduated at or near the top of their class.

"Shirley was a homemaker. She raised the kids. Did all the cooking, she can really cook! And all the sewing. That was her love. And her church. She was just an excellent mother."

Roy's practice continued to thrive but his attempt at farming became his albatross. Roy wasn't the only farmer that had heard dairy's siren song and the price of milk kept declining due to the huge surplus of milk and milk producers. Roy had mortgages, loans on machinery and bills from running the operation and there was no sign of improvement on the horizon. It began to dawn on him that he could face bankruptcy.

Fortunately for Roy, the federal government introduced a program to encourage some farmers to stop producing milk. Roy jumped all over it, selling his cattle and equipment for pennies on the dollar in order to avoid losing everything. He had been saved from financial disaster but his farming days were done. He turned his farm buildings into winter storage for boats and when his children had grown up and moved on, put the farm up for sale. But getting out of the land turned out to have additional unforeseen difficulties.

"It might have taken about five years or a little longer before we finally found someone to buy the house. Then the land. We sold off a lot of smaller pieces to farmers. The main chunk took awhile to sell. Probably the scariest deal was—again, I'm not a good business person—a guy who was a real shyster came to me and said, 'I want to buy your place, but I want to rent it first.' I had this lawyer draw up this elaborate renting deal and for about eight months he paid the rent every month on time. Then all of a sudden I couldn't get the rent out of him. And then he sued me for all kinds of stuff, claiming that the rent payment he had been paying me each month was actually money that was supposed to go towards purchasing. He comes with his lawyer into court with copies of his checks and on them is written 'lease to buy payment' which I said was never on there when he sent them to me. 'Well prove it,' he said."

Roy was stymied. As a town doctor, Roy's role was to look out for people. He protected and respected their secrets, ailments and struggles. He knew a little bit extra about everyone around and he never used it against them, never held it over anyone nor judged them. Roy always assumed the best in people, which often caught him on the wrong side of business dealings. But in the long run, he always felt doing the right thing would come back around. And by earning his patients' trust, Roy caught just such a break.

"I come to find out one of my patients was the president of the Cadillac State Bank which was the bank we used. And one

day, kind of a miracle, he came into the office to see me a week before I had to go into court before the judge and get this thing hashed out. I told him, this guy is a crook and I told him about the checks. And he says, 'You got no problem. We photograph every check when it goes through and I can call down to the main office and get photocopies of the checks.' Sure enough, the next day I got these in my hand and none of that 'lease to buy' stuff was on them. So I went before the judge and this other guy's giving all these statements and spiel. And my lawyer asks if we can approach the bench. We showed the judge the checks that were deposited in the bank, with none of that on there. And of course the judge just threw it out."

Due to the financial losses he suffered from his farming and sale of his property, Roy wasn't able to retire. He continued to run his small practice and he and Shirley moved into a small home in Cadillac. But there was an upside to all of it—without the burden of the farm and with his kids grown, Roy had time for golf again.

Ten years after his initial round with Dr. Jim Johnson, Roy took his friend up on his offer and joined Crystal Downs Country Club in 1986. It was that same summer while playing in the Buick Open in Michigan that Ben Crenshaw, a passionate student of golf architecture, journeyed up to Crystal Downs. Crenshaw left stunned by Mackenzie's design and began publicly singing its praises.

It might have been news to the world but Roy already knew he was joining one of the great courses in the world. He had no idea, however, that he was about to begin one of the great friendships of his life, a friendship that would make possible his remarkable journey as a senior amateur golfer.

You gotta put it on the road if you want to be any good. You gotta get out there and play in stuff. You gotta lose so you can figure out how to win.
— Fred Muller
Head Professional
Crystal Downs Country Club

12

The Head Pro: Fred Muller

Simply put, the rest of this story wouldn't have happened without Fred Muller.

In addition to spectacular settings, great courses tend to have unique head professionals. While serving the interests of the membership, these club pros are the unsung heroes whose encouragement, patient lessons and behind-the-scene actions plant the seeds of happiness that golfers sow the rest of their lives.

After playing for Georgia State University, Fred competed on the PGA, Australasian and South American Tours which included winning the Michigan Open in 1981, the 60th Anniversary of Walter Hagen's victory.

Fred became the head pro at Crystal Downs in 1977, around the same time Roy played the course for the first time. Fred's passion for golf architecture and travel combined with his successful playing resumé gave him much to draw from in his lessons with members. Around the time Roy joined the club in the mid-1980s, Fred helped launch Crystal Downs member Tom Doak's golf architecture career when he recommended Doak for his first design job in nearby Traverse City. A decade later, Doak had cemented his place in the renaissance of classic golf design and it was coincidentally at Crystal Downs where the visionary developer, Mike Keiser, agreed to engage Doak to design what became the highly regarded Pacific Dunes course in Bandon, Oregon.

Back in 1987, Fred was about to have a comparable impact on Roy's life as they became fast friends. Fred took the older Roy under his wing with Roy's unassuming nature playing the perfect straight man for Fred's razor-sharp wit. Fred taught Roy course management. How to grind, to play the shot at hand and not to quit if he made a couple double bogeys. But before Roy could take his game on the road, he had to solve his putting woes. The greens at Crystal Downs were more difficult than any Roy had ever faced and required enormous skill. He had always been a good long-distance putter but struggled with shorter putts.

Roy's homemade putter

One day he played with an eye doctor who surmised the problem might be his perception from the side of the putting line. Roy started experimenting putting "sidesaddle" facing the hole like he'd seen Sam Snead putt, as you would if you were going to roll the ball to the hole with your hand.

Roy could see the line better and his putting improved immediately. But then his back started hurting so he decided to tinker with a longer putter. Roy researched legal grip placement, found a putter head he liked—a peculiar T-shaped head that looked like a bullet shell with a flat face attached to it—and inserted an old driver shaft into it.

For the next couple of years, he carried two putters—the

conventional one with a normal stance for long putts and the longer putter used sidesaddle for short putts. Eventually, Roy ditched the conventional putter and converted to the long putter, putting everything sidesaddle.

The missing piece, found. He could already drive for show. Now he could putt for dough.

Combining his carefree nature and simple approach to the game—have fun, respect the game and your competitors—Roy quickly found that he was competitive with top senior amateurs who had been playing their entire lives. Given his age, his lack of tournament experience, his full-time job and the extremely short playing season in Northern Michigan, Roy was more than holding his own. But there's a very small window for elite senior amateur players. The major senior amateur tournaments require players to be 55 years old and by their early 60's, it's tough for them to compete against the players just a few years younger. Roy wasn't able to beat the best senior players but he was competitive and as he got older, into his 60's, he started beating them. They were falling back and he was still improving.

Roy's first big win was the American Senior Match Play in Florida in 1995 at 63 years old where he beat the 3rd and 6th-ranked seniors in the nation. While his peers were retiring and losing their touch, Roy kept practicing medicine and making putts. He qualified for his first USGA Senior Amateur in 1998 at Skokie Country Club in Illinois at 66 years old. He qualified a second time, shooting his age (72) to qualify for the 2004 USGA Senior Amateur at Bel-Air Country Club in Los Angeles in which he lost in a playoff to advance to match play.

The next year, Roy shot his age again (73) to qualify for the 2005 USGA Senior Amateur at The Farm Golf Club in Georgia. This time, Roy got over the hump and qualified for match play. He drew a formidable first round opponent, Jack Vardaman, one of the top senior players in the nation and a multiple-time club champion at Congressional Country Club, who had lost in the quarterfinals of the Senior Amateur the year before. Roy went into the last hole with a 1-Up lead and made par after lagging a 30-foot putt close. Standing on the 18th green waiting for Vardaman to stroke his must-make 25-foot downhill putt, Roy was already celebrating inside that he'd beat the big gun. When Vardaman rolled in his big-breaking putt to even the match and force extra holes, Roy was in shock and promptly lost the match on the 19th hole. Vardaman went all the way to the semi-finals before losing to that year's champion while Roy headed home with Fred's words ringing true...

"You gotta lose so you can figure out how to win."

13

When Bad Things Happen To Good People

While Roy was learning how to bounce-back on the golf course, life tossed him another setback.

Around the time he turned 70, Roy received an unexpected call. A large medical group wanted to buy out his McBain practice, his life's work. Roy reasoned that perhaps it was time for him to hang it up.

Long gone were the early days of Roy's career when he did all of his own surgeries. Insurance and lawsuits ruled the day.

"When I came to Cadillac, we didn't have any specialists. You had to do your own surgery. If you couldn't do it, your buddy in the next town would teach you how to do it. That's the way it was way back then. You used to be able to do a lot of procedures in the emergency room. Guy's got a little cyst on his hand that you wanted to take off—I used to do that in the emergency room. Give a little local, take it off, put a couple stitches in. Used to be

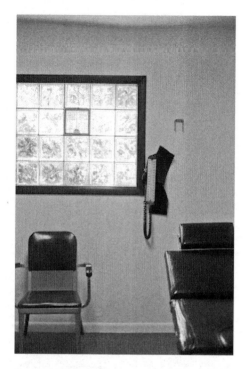

Roy's examining room

doctors could have your own lab in the office where you drew your own blood and you'd train one of your people to test it whether it be for lipids or all the blood chemistry. Now you ship everything out."

Selling his practice was a chance to slow down and after the financial losses they had suffered from their farming miscues, it would finally provide Roy and Shirley with a simple, comfortable retirement. But Roy's trusting nature and lack of business instincts led him to enter into what was little more than a handshake agreement in return for a small down payment with the bulk of the funds to be paid a year later. Some of those in the medical group were long-term friends and acquaintances Roy trusted so he didn't think twice about the deal.

At the end of the year, the group contacted Roy and asked for another six months to pay, to which he agreed. Then they asked for another six months and again Roy agreed. But then he began to hear rumors that the medical group had sold their business to a large hospital chain. Roy attempted to inquire about his money and his calls went unreturned. The money had been distributed to the group members and the business that purchased Roy's practice had been dissolved. Roy's money was gone and due to the nature of the agreement he entered into, Roy had no recourse.

It turned out to be a financial disaster from which he and Shirley have yet to recover.

Roy had been depending on the payment to retire and couldn't afford to slow down as planned. But he didn't spend much time fretting. Didn't dwell on the negatives or harbor ill will. He'd been working his entire life, he'd just keep on going. Fortunately, he had kept the Marion office so he returned to his practice where he's still seeing patients to this day.

And while others may have taken advantage of Roy, he always put his patients first. He gave physicals at a discount, waived bills that couldn't be paid and in over 40 years of practicing medicine, with over 20,000 patients cared for, Roy was never sued by a single one of them.

The breaks will even themselves up in the
long run—if the run is long enough.
– Bobby Jones

14

Life To The Fullest

2005–2010

Roy's trophy case

Roy kept seeing patients, spending time with his family and playing golf as the world changed rapidly around him. He was immensely proud of his grown children who had found success in such challenging fields as nuclear power, mathematics and medicine while starting families of their own. Roy watched in amazement as his six grandchildren embraced the technological revolution and companies like Apple, Amazon, Facebook, Google, Microsoft, Twitter and YouTube transformed how people communicated and were entertained. Roy was a long way from the days of raising his kids with Shirley in a log cabin during med school. In many ways, however, he still approached his life the same way.

He was often asked by friends and fellow members why he was still working. While most were unaware of his financial needs, there was more to it for Roy than the money.

"It makes me get up in the morning. And the people I see are people I've known since they were kids or I delivered them."

People like Marlene, who'd been Roy's assistant since he hired her out of high school in 1968.

Golf trips to warmer climates helped him get through the long Michigan winters and a round with Arnold Palmer at Tradition Golf Club in La Quinta, California on one such trip gave Roy a memory for a lifetime.

A more personal highlight occurred when Roy journeyed back to Japan for the first time since he had left in handcuffs to reunite with his old pal, Matsumoto. Roy took a special gift with him—Matsumoto's championship trophy he had held onto all those years. Matsumoto joyfully accepted the trophy but insisted Roy return home with another memento.

For the most part, though, Roy stuck around Northern Michigan. And by 2010, the world felt upside down. He'd watched with sadness as companies disappeared and industries

Roy's Arnold Palmer memorabilia

moved away from the small Michigan towns around him. The reeling economy had Michigan against the ropes and those small towns were barely hanging on. The days of Palmer and Nicklaus that had inspired Roy's friends to build the local muni were long gone. Private jets transported players around the globe to launch 350-yard drives on stretched-out courses while tabloids invaded the sport.

Another summer started and amateur golfers everywhere enjoyed the annual tradition of playing in club, local, state, regional, national and invitational tournaments to measure themselves against the course and their opponents and to experience the satisfaction of striving and trying to deliver. Junior golfers aspiring to play in high school and college. Collegiate golfers aspiring to play professionally. Mid-Amateurs (25 and over), Senior Amateurs (55 and over) and Super Senior

Roy's Katsuaki Matsumoto poster

Amateurs (65 and over) juggling life, work and family in pursuit of their personal best.

While most 78-year-olds had accepted their best days were behind them and resigned themselves to playing the forward tees, Roy was feeling good about his game. He'd won over 20 amateur tournaments, giving him ample confidence he could close the deal when he got in contention.

Roy teeing off #2 at Crystal Downs Country Club

Roy putting on #4 at Crystal Downs Country Club

Two key things kept him competitive. He hit the ball as far, if not farther, than guys much younger. And he could putt with the best of them.

Distance and accuracy. Two great equalizers to keep Father Time at bay. But Roy had another advantage over his competition—his spirit. Even though he was capable of playing to a high level and had the trophies to prove it, his approach to the game was constantly fun and carefree. He saw every round as a gift and considered it a privilege to have the time, health and opportunity to enjoy the game. While others worked at and struggled with their games, Roy just played. No ego, no fears, no embarrassment, no gloating. He loved the unpredictable twists, turns and bounces that came with every round. He laughed at his bad shots, shrugging off the duffs without letting them get to him. He never let any shot mean more than what it was—a chance to pick the right club and do something special.

And while the rules of the game only permit 14 clubs, every golfer brings another club to the tee, what sports psychologist Dr. Bob Rotella dubs, "Your 15th Club."

If your 15th Club is forged with all of the moments of your past, your successes and failures, confidence and doubt, and your collective memories that manifest in the form of nerves that can focus or distract...then Roy's 15th Club was as strong as anyone's.

15

I Found Something

Wednesday, July 15th, 2010

Roy was looking forward to playing Crystal Downs that day. It was an opportunity to tee it up with one of his good friends and it was a stunningly clear, brisk Northern Michigan summer day. The type of day someone who's been through a Michigan winter never takes for granted.

Golf had been fickle for Roy so far that summer. His swing had been inconsistent and he had begun to wonder if his early-season optimism had been unfounded. Perhaps time was catching up.

But a week earlier, something clicked. For the love of competition, Roy decided to play in the Michigan Senior Open despite struggling with his game. Warming up before the first round he found something with his elbow position and after 18 holes, 78-year-old Roy was the tournament leader. But midway through the second round in 90-degree-plus heat, Roy's heart started to flutter and he withdrew. He had unknowingly suffered a heart attack a number of years earlier while playing in a tournament in Mexico and hadn't said anything until he started fading on the flight home. As soon as he'd landed in Traverse City, Ed had taken him straight to the hospital where they discovered he was in heart failure and put in a stint. Roy decided this time not to press his luck. While disappointed to withdraw, he was relieved to discover he was only feeling the effects of heat exhaustion or sunstroke and he left the tournament excited that he'd been able to carry over what he found on the range to the first round.

Now standing on the 1st tee at Crystal Downs with confidence rejuvenated, Roy ripped his drive from the back markers and proclaimed that he was going to try and play in the Club Championship at the end of the month.

Because you never know what might happen.

And you can't win if you don't play.

16

Club Championship Qualifying

Friday, July 23rd, 2010

Roy & his caddie, Gaby Muller

The qualifying round for the Crystal Downs Club Championship was 18 holes of stroke play from the back tees at scratch (no handicap strokes). The low 15 players and defending champion would be seeded into match play brackets like the Sweet Sixteen in NCAA basketball's March Madness. First round Saturday morning, quarterfinals Saturday afternoon, semi-finals Sunday morning and finals Sunday afternoon. Five competitive rounds in three days for the finalists.

With the pressure of competition amplifying the challenge of putting at Crystal Downs, it was easy to wear out the nerves. All told, winning the tournament was a tiring weekend for the champion and would seemingly be an overwhelming task for Roy. But he saw it as a chance to have fun. A chance to be a kid and play the game he loved.

The hopeful qualifiers were greeted with a blustery day, the wind blowing off Lake Michigan adding an additional degree of difficulty to an already challenging course. Good scores would not come easily.

Roy was ready. He had his bag of assorted clubs he'd picked up along the way. His magic putter. And his trusted caddie, Gaby, Fred Muller's 17-year-old daughter, herself a strong player on the way to play for Michigan State University.

Roy ripped his driver on the elevated tee of the 460-yard par 4 1st hole and immediately turned to Gaby, his eyes for the tournament.

"Where'd it go?"

"Down the middle, about 280," she replied.

Roy's eyesight had started to fade due to glaucoma and he had trouble following the ball as far as he could hit it so he relied on Gaby to keep an eye on his shots. She'd serve an additional role in match play, telling Roy where his opponent stood since Roy couldn't see where his opponent's shots went, either.

"And it's so important when you play match play to know where your opponent is. I want to know where his ball is. He's not going to tell me 'I got a bad lie.' So I had her spot the ball and tell me where they were and all this and that. And she's a good golfer too, so she encouraged me."

About four hours later, Roy quickly surveyed an 8-foot putt on the 18th green and calmly rolled the ball into the center of the hole, giving him a 75, the second lowest score of the qualifying round. Roy was seeded 3rd behind Kelly Robinson, a former collegiate player for Rollins College who had carded a 73, and the top-seeded defending champion who was exempt from qualifying.

With the prospect of back-to-back days of 36 holes facing the two players who made the finals, the other qualifiers went to the practice range or home to rest in anticipation of the long tournament weekend. But Roy headed back to the first tee to host two guests as a favor to a fellow member and friend.

Feeling great about his game, he shot 74 in the afternoon, leaving the guests laughing and shaking their heads in amazement as they struggled to break 90.

17

First Two Rounds Of Match Play

Saturday, July 24th, 2010

While professional golf today is almost exclusively stroke play, most major amateur tournaments still feature a match play format. Whereas a golfer counts every shot in stroke play, match play is a head-to-head battle between opponents in which each hole is a competition in itself to be halved, won or lost. The player who wins the most holes is the winner of the match. In a match where both golfers are playing well and evenly matched, it often comes down to a single hole. Sometimes it comes down to a mistake, a spectacular shot or a bit of luck. Late in a close match when few holes remain to be played, momentum can shift suddenly, creating enormous pressure on a player.

The drama of match play is heightened by the nature and character of the golf course where it takes place. A golf course that requires a variety of shots, where mistakes are easy to make and severely punished, and where a player can never relax, often brings out the best in match play competition.

Crystal Downs checks all those boxes

The breeze was up again Saturday morning as the players warmed up for their first match. Roy completed his practice session in his trademark style—he slowly put four balls on tees in a perfect line, took his driver and whacked each one long and straight. Even though he couldn't see the balls once they sailed into the trees at the end of the range, he knew by feel how well he hit them and where they were going. He didn't bother to look up that morning after each swing, the feel told him all he needed to know—the contact with the ball was dead-center in the sweet spot.

Roy's first match was against Chad Daniels, a good player from Houston who hit it a mile. Roy struck the ball purely, his normally great putting was on a deadly level of accuracy and he won his first match handily.

Roy stayed in the zone against Al Zimmerman that afternoon in the quarterfinals, driving the ball beautifully and making putts. Roy jumped off to a large early lead and closed the match out on the 15th hole.

While he'd breezed through his first day, Sunday loomed as a much tougher challenge. The seedings had held and Roy's opponent in the semi-final match was the #2 seed, three-time club champion and one of the top two players in the club, Kelly Robinson.

18

The Semi-Finals

Sunday, July 25th, 2010

Kelly Robinson was an experienced and skilled tournament player who carried a plus handicap despite having a successful career and young family. Roy considered Kelly a much better golfer but wasn't intimidated. Roy felt his hot putter could even things up, leaving Kelly with only one small advantage—he was over 40 years younger than Roy.

Fred Muller didn't say anything to Roy but he didn't share his confidence. *Roy had played 36 holes Friday and two matches Saturday. Kelly is way too good, no way he is going to beat him,* thought Fred. *Even if Roy did pull off the upset, he'd be overmatched in the final against the likely top-seed.*

But as Roy finished warming up for his match on the putting green, he quietly discovered one more advantage. A game-changing advantage.

"I'm a little superstitious about things. I talk to the golf ball.

ne...

If it's good, if it's kind. If I have a golf ball that goes in the sand trap three times, I take it out of the bag, I don't play it anymore. Because you just know it's unlucky. I never play a golf ball that I found even though it's a brand new ball. I figure that ball got lost by somebody so it's an unlucky ball. And I don't play with a Number 3 ball. My most lucky number is 2 so I made sure I had some #2 golf balls. And sure enough this one, I knew. I just had a premonition this was going to be a lucky ball that day. I got on the practice putting green and I'm making everything. This ball was going in like a gopher going down a hole."

Roy headed down to the first tee where he and Kelly chatted before teeing off. It was a beautiful morning with a few scattered clouds. The wind was up again and a bit stronger than Saturday, enough to add that extra dimension that makes for a great test of golf. Roy thought about how lucky he was to be there. How much he enjoyed the competition and especially playing with Kelly since he really admired his game.

They teed off and were on their way.

Through the early holes Roy and Kelly both hit the ball solidly. Though the wind made scoring a challenge, they didn't allow it to affect them mentally. Making their way through the first nine holes battling the wind, something unexpected began to happen...

Kelly fell behind as Roy buried every critical putt, quickly gaining a 2-Up advantage. Kelly had witnessed Roy's putting streaks before in casual rounds and knew it could mean trouble. Despite playing well, Kelly realized he'd have to make some birdies in the tough conditions to have a chance. He wasn't panicked but couldn't afford to fall farther behind. And as much as he loved Roy, he was determined not to get beat by a 78-year-old. Kelly stayed focused and continued hitting good shots...

And watched Roy pull further ahead. 3-Up. 4-Up.

On the 14th hole, Roy calmly drained an 8-foot birdie putt. The match was over.

Walking into the clubhouse barely two and a half hours after the match had begun, everyone assumed the brief duration meant Kelly had won easily. Before anyone could ask, Kelly announced to the room, "I didn't just lose to a 78-year-old, I got annihilated by a 78-year-old. And I played well."

The members exchanged looks of surprise as the room started to buzz.

Accepting congratulations, Roy demurred, "Kelly played great. I just got real lucky. I had a lucky golf ball."

His comment was greeted with chuckles, the usual response Roy gets whenever he credits luck for his success. But Roy didn't laugh, he was completely serious.

He knew he had a lucky ball.

In the other semi-final match, the #1 seed, defending champion, 9-time club champion and course record-holder won handily. All that stood between Roy and the club championship was the best player in the club, his son, Dr. Edward Chase Vomastek.

After a quick lunch, Ed headed down to the range to hit a few balls and stay loose. Roy had a different plan he shared with Fred, "I'm going to go out to my van and take a nap. Can you have someone come out and wake me up a few minutes before we tee off?"

"Do you want enough time to hit some balls before you tee off?" Fred asked.

"Nah. I just need to close my eyes for a few minutes."

Fred shook his head as several members in the room laughed. But Roy wasn't kidding. Exhausted from his morning match and the previous two days of competitive golf, he went to his van in the parking lot, cranked back his seat and took a nap.

Roy's infamous van

Roy had bought the van a few years earlier for his golf equipment and fishing gear and also so he could pull off the road and nap when driving back home to Northern Michigan after tournaments in the summer. Roy found it in Texas on eBay. A tiny used car dealer had bought it at an auction and couldn't sell it. The blue book was $15,000, Roy bought it for $6,000. He flew down to Texas and drove it back to Michigan where he affixed the license plate he'd had for twenty years—SCRATCH.

By 12:30pm, Roy was sound asleep and snoring.

Harry Vardon always said,
'No matter what happens,
keep on hitting the ball'.
— Bobby Jones

Hit the ball and knock it in the hole.
– Roy Vomastek

—————————

19

The Championship Match

Sunday, July 25th, 2010

Ed & Roy Vomastek

"Wake up, Dr. Roy! Ten minutes! Gotta go!" Gaby pounded on the door of Roy's van.

Roy stirred, turned off the bluegrass music, lumbered out of the van and headed to the first tee to meet his son.

Roy and Ed had met three times before in the Crystal Downs Club Championship with Roy winning once and Ed winning the other two. They were best friends with the differences in their personalities and style of play providing perfect foils for each other.

Ed's work as an anesthesiologist required precision and the elimination of chance to whatever extent possible which carried over to his approach to golf. He analyzed everything within his control. Depending on the wind, he might change the makeup of his bag, substituting a club in anticipation of specific shots the prevailing wind might require. The firmness of the greens would cause him to change his golf ball selection for the round. His clubs were always the latest technology, everything custom-fitted for his swing. A workshop in his garage enabled him to switch shafts, change grips, adjust lofts and make repairs. He knew his swing speed, launch angle and ball speed with every club and loved the technical aspects of the game.

Watching Ed play was often a wonderful study in ball striking and course management. He consistently played Crystal Downs better than anyone in the history of the course. He knew where the danger was, could spot opportunity and usually hit the required shot. He knew where to hit it and where not to. Mistakes were rare and small and almost always allowing for recovery which made him a formidable opponent in match play.

Ed's intensity had been fostered during his youth. The early years in the log cabin when Roy and Shirley were scraping by. The early mornings in high school when he had to wake up before school to milk the cows, a chore that had sliced off a tip of one of his fingers. And then Ed's competitive nature driving him to play golf and cajole his dad back into playing and competing with him.

He shared a close bond with his dad not only from their times spent together on the course but also through experiencing some near-misses off of it. Roy had performed Ed's emergency appendectomy when Ed was a kid. And they'd brushed against death together while flying across Lake Michigan one day when Roy had flown down to Missouri to pick Ed up from college. An air controller sent them straight into a terrible storm with rain so strong they couldn't see an inch past the windshield. Water was coming through the air vents, lightning cracked all around them. They were hitting air pockets and dropping 500 feet at a time causing the autopilot to keep bouncing off. When the air controller told them to maintain course, Roy refused, swore louder than Ed had ever heard him and turned straight west back out into the lake, gambling that the storm was lake-effect. His dad's instincts paid off and five minutes later they broke free into safer sky. To this day, Ed calls it the scariest moment of his life and still can't believe they survived.

Roy had raised a tough competitor and if he was going to beat his son, he couldn't depend on Ed playing poorly. He'd have to play better. And he'd have to play his own style.

Roy's approach to the game and his equipment were the complete opposite of Ed's. Golf ball selection came down to which one felt lucky. Clubs selected on a whim. He didn't know his clubhead speed and didn't really care. His game was less about course management and more about hitting the shot he saw in each given moment resulting in sometimes crazy and often spectacular shots.

As Fred explained once after Roy performed well in a

tournament, "Roy, the key for you today was that you played your stupid shots extremely well."

But the real joy in Roy's game came from putting sidesaddle with his homemade long putter. No alignment marks on the ball, no practice strokes. When Roy was away and first to putt, he often wouldn't even mark his ball and replace it. He'd just study the line, step up, stroke the ball and watch it roll beautifully, end-over-end to its appointed destiny with the bottom of the cup.

Willie Park, Jr., the legendary 19th century Scotsman, two-time Open Champion, golf club maker, course architect and author of the first book about golf written by a professional golfer, is famous for succinctly stating, "A man who can putt is a match for anyone."

Roy Vomastek is living proof.

Ed knew he was the better player. But he also knew not to take his dad lightly. As father and son headed to the first tee for their match, they both had ample perspective. They knew where they'd been and how fortunate they were. They both owed their success to each other and whoever won would credit the other as inspiring their victory.

20

Hole #1 - 460 Yards - Par 4

As Roy reached the tee, other than Fred Muller and a couple of caddies who loved Roy and were tagging along to watch, there were no other spectators.

Ed looked at Fred with a laugh, "I know there isn't a single person rooting for me and I don't blame them. And if you are wondering why I'm not taking a caddie, it's because I know I can't trust any of them when I play my dad."

Then the needles came out like they always did when Roy and Ed played together.

"Pa, you going to be able to stand up for 18 holes?"

"What makes you think it's going to take me that long to finish you off? By the way, Ed, when are Tam and the girls going to get here? I enjoy them rooting against you."

Roy was referring to Ed's wife and young daughters, Roy's grandchildren, but Ed didn't take the bait. He was ready to get going.

"Pa, I'm playing a Pro V1 with my usual red lines."

"I've got a Titleist NXT number 2."

It was the same lucky ball Roy had rolled to victory in his semi-final match.

While Roy continued to look at his lucky ball, Ed experienced a bucketful of emotions. Each time he played with his dad it was one more round deducted from a too-quickly declining balance in an account that could never be replenished. He wanted to enjoy every second of the experience. He knew he'd enjoy it even more by winning convincingly. There would be no casual play, no soft-heartedness in the match from Ed and he knew he wouldn't see any let-up from his dad, either. Roy and Ed's friendship was built around competition, never giving an inch while pushing each other to excel. Adding to Ed's motivation was one additional factor—he didn't want to be the fourth and final player in the 2010 Club Championship to be beat by a 78-year-old.

The elevated 1st tee provides a spectacular view of the front nine holes with Crystal Lake shimmering in the distance. The sheer beauty of the hole often has visitors reaching for their camera as they realize they're about to experience a course of architectural genius that continues to stand the test of time.

Despite the beauty of the hole, one can't be seduced for long. While golf course architects often provide a gentle beginning to a round with a relatively easy opening hole, MacKenzie was in no such frame of mind when he designed Crystal Downs. The first hole is one of the hardest holes on the course. Tall fescue lines both sides of the fairway and an elongated fairway bunker on the right side collects errant drives. The green blends into a natural plateau, sloping severely right-to-left and back-to-front. A shot finishing above the hole virtually guarantees a three-putt and sometimes worse.

The sky was bright blue with scattered clouds. The wind, having strengthened from the morning round, blew from the south, presenting an additional factor for the Championship match as the hole was playing directly into the wind and longer than the 460 yards on the scorecard despite being considerably downhill.

Ed hit first and pushed his drive right into the first cut of rough where it took a hard bounce over the bunker into the fescue.

Roy teed up his ball, stepped into his stance and took a rip at it.

"Where'd it go?" he asked Gaby.

"Down the middle, Dr. Roy."

And they were off.

Roy reached his ball and watched from across the fairway as Ed studied his ball, tangled in the thick rough. His only option was to chip his wedge sideways and hope to hit his third shot close. Still facing a 200-yard shot into the wind, Ed had to play his third shot before Roy had played his second. Ed nailed his hybrid over the back edge of the green leaving a chip that would be near-impossible to keep on the green.

With Ed in serious trouble, Roy figured bogey was likely to win the hole. He grabbed his hybrid, knowing he had to keep it below the hole. Roy's shot landed just short and left of the green in the rough, an ideal spot. After Ed's chip ran far from the hole, Roy pitched his on. Ed missed his bogey putt and Roy lagged his par putt close.

Roy had drawn first blood and was 1-Up in the final match.

21

Hole #2 - 425 Yards - Par 4

The layout of the first two holes creates an interesting combination for the start of rounds. The prevailing winds tend to come from either north or south, resulting in one of the first two holes dead into the wind, the other straight downwind. Capitalizing on the downwind hole is critical since you pay the price on the hole into the wind.

The second hole plays uphill the entire way alongside the downhill first, rising to a green with the greatest degree of slope from back-to-front of any green on the course. MacKenzie disguised the severity of the rise by placing the tee box on a slightly elevated plateau and the green to the left of a small fescue covered hill, fronted by a bunker. Like the first hole, the fairway is lined with high fescue grass on both sides, ever-ready to devour errant tee shots.

Roy wanted to capitalize on winning the 1st hole and get off to a strong start. The helping wind and a good drive would leave him a mid-iron to the green. Addressing the ball, Roy settled into a balanced stance, turned and swung. Feeling the contact, he knew it was pulled and heading loft. He turned to Gaby.

"It's in the high stuff," she confirmed.

Ed promptly capitalized, sending his drive long and up the middle of the fairway, the ball settling no more than a short iron from the green.

Roy located his ball quickly in the high grass and fortunately had a decent lie, enabling him to advance the ball but not reach the green. He punched his 9-iron and it rolled to a stop 40 yards short of the green. A smart play, he was still in the hole.

Ed knew he needed to leave his approach below the hole. His 8-iron landed short and right of the hole, spun and stopped 10 feet from the cup.

Seeing Ed's shot, Roy figured Ed would make par at worst. He needed to get up-and-down and hope Ed missed to eke out a halve. Roy knew if he carried his shot slightly past a ridge on the green it would feed toward the hole and possibly get close…difficult but doable. His hot putter could escape with a tie. Roy's pitch wasn't as crisp as he wanted—the ball rolled partly up the ridge, then retreated to a stop 20 feet from the hole. Disappointing shot.

Studying his difficult and significantly breaking 20-footer up the ridge, Roy lined up quickly and stroked his par putt. His ball tracked up the ridge and broke directly toward the hole—veering offline at the last second and sliding past the edge.

Ed let out a quiet sigh of relief—he had fully expected his dad to make the challenging putt. Ed lagged his putt close for a conceded par to win the hole.

All-Square after two holes.

22

Hole #3 - 191 Yards - Par 3

Standing on the tee, it was Roy's turn to be unhappy with his play on the previous hole. He hadn't struck a single shot well, not even his chip, and knew he couldn't play that way and have any chance of winning. Then Roy looked on the bright side—he had nearly made par, almost halving the hole with a great putt. His putter was working, he just needed good swings with the other clubs.

Playing 191 yards downhill, the 3rd hole makes club selection tricky. The wind tends to quarter into the player from the left or away from the right, an effect that can be as much as two clubs. The green angles from right-to-left, well-protected by bunkers short and long with the green tucked against the bottom of a towering exposed dune behind it.

The south wind was quartering against them so Ed flighted his 4-iron with a low draw against the wind toward the back left flag location. His ball landed left-center and tracked to a stop 12 feet from the hole.

Roy's hybrid ballooned in the wind and came down short and right of the green. He followed with an uncharacteristically poor chip, leaving another 20-foot putt for par. The hole he was digging had gotten deeper. Ed liked his chances to win the hole as he watched his dad grab his putter and walk onto the green.

By the time Roy found the line, he had already let go of his first two shots on the hole. Taking little time, he addressed his ball and stroked the putt...which rolled directly into the center of the cup, rattling to the bottom for a par.

Ed shook his head—he'd seen his dad do that too many times to remember. He now had 12 feet for birdie to win the hole. Ed's putt rolled perfectly, tracking toward the center of the cup...and slid by the hole. Roy had dodged his first bullet.

All-Square through three.

23

Hole #4 - 409 Yards - Par 4

A dogleg left-to-right with a fairway sloping the opposite right-to-left. Trees lining the right side, high fescue the left. The hole was playing back into the south wind and set up perfectly for Ed's preferred fade with his driver which is exactly what he did, smacking his drive up the left-center of the fairway and leaving himself a mid-iron for his slightly uphill second shot.

Roy continued his struggles off the tee, pulling his drive left. The ball hit the ground hard and bounced towards the fescue in an area that often resulted in lost balls. Roy looked at Gaby who frowned and shrugged, uncertain of his ball's fate.

They headed towards the line they'd last seen it on and came upon the lucky ball resting in the first cut of rough, three inches from the high fescue. Instead of a lost ball or having to punch out sideways, Roy had a clear shot to the green, 190 yards away.

The 4th green sits slightly elevated protected by a huge bunker front left and a false front in the middle and right that sends a short shot back down the hill, leaving a difficult chip. Roy swung hybrid for the long uphill shot into the wind and pulled it towards the dreaded bunker on the left.

His ball landed just shy of the bunker and skirted around the edge then took an inexplicable bounce over the back part of the bunker before coming to rest in the rough on the left side of the green. A relatively easy uphill chip remained to get in position for an unlikely par.

Ed looked at his dad in shock, "What was that?"

Roy turned to Gaby and smiled, "Lucky ball."

Ed fired his 5-iron at the middle of the green, bringing his shot in low against the wind and leaving himself a 15-foot birdie putt. Another textbook shot.

Roy chipped his ball to the spot he wanted to below the hole, leaving himself an uphill five-footer for par if Ed didn't make his birdie.

Ed knew he couldn't get too aggressive with his putt and risk running it several feet by the hole. He lagged his putt to tap-in range for a conceded par. The pressure was back on Roy and his must-make par save.

Roy wasted no time, selected his line and buried the putt in the middle of the hole.

All-Square after four holes.

24

Hole #5 - 353 Yards - Par 4

The players walked off the green and up the steps to the tee of the hole widely regarded as one of Alister MacKenzie's greatest and most complicated holes—*Golf Magazine's* project to identify the top 100 holes in the world included the 5th at Crystal Downs. Although playing only 353 yards, the 5th is fraught with challenges. The tee shot on the sharp dogleg-left must skirt the edge of a giant oak bordering the right side and carry a large crest in the middle of the fairway down to a blind landing area, leaving a short iron from an uneven lie to a green that slopes dramatically from left-to-right. The 5th is also the most heavily bunkered hole on the course with a total of nine bunkers, including the "Three Sisters" bunkers cut into the hillside bordering the left of the hole. Miss your drive too far right and you'll find the fescue. Too far left and you won't clear the hillside, likely ending up in the fescue or bunkers. Even a straight drive often kicks through the fairway into the rough.

Ed hit another perfect drive up the right side of the fairway, leaving an ideal approach angle to the green.

Roy teed his ball up, tried to settle down and find his tempo He felt like he hadn't hit a good shot since the first hole but his putter and some luck had kept him level. He swung and drove it solidly into the fairway, close to Ed's ball.

Despite only having wedges into the green, their approach shots called for unusual precision with the added challenge of both Roy and Ed's balls resting below their feet. The slope of the green had a half-bowl effect in the middle that could result in a shot to the middle of the green rolling all the way down to a bunker on the right. Both Roy and Ed knew the play was to the left side of the green to get to the hole cut on the back shelf but missing the green left would virtually guarantee a bogey.

Ed hit his wedge to the left-center of the green leaving a 15-foot uphill putt from the bowl for birdie. Roy decided to try and hit his wedge all the way to the back shelf and caught it too solidly. His ball carried over the green leaving a chip shot that would be impossible to stop near the hole. Sure enough, his chip rolled down the slope of the green and settled 25 feet away, outside of Ed's birdie putt. Roy missed his par save and Ed lagged it close for a winning par.

Roy kicked himself inside for the careless bogey as he headed towards the 6th tee, trailing for the first time in the match.

Roy was 1-Down through five holes.

25

Hole #6 - 384 Yards - Par 4

Roy shifted his focus to positive thoughts as he waited for Ed to tee off.

You'll find the groove. Just keep swinging, keep playing the shots.

Since his hiccup on the first hole, Ed had reeled off four steady pars, hitting every fairway and green. Roy knew he was going to have play solidly to keep the match close.

The 6th hole incorporates MacKenzie's idea of a forced carry. The tee shot must pass the crest of a hill or it will roll backward some 50 yards down the hill leaving the player a long, blind second shot. A towering tree guards the right side of the fairway. To the right of the tree, the "Scabs" bunkers appear to give you an aiming line for a shortcut to the green in the distance of the dogleg-right but they're a deception—a patch of high fescue lies hidden beyond the Scabs.

Ed drove his ball down the middle of the fairway, easily

cresting the hill and leaving a short iron to the green. Roy hit another mediocre shot, barely making the crest of the hill and settling into the left rough. He was having a hard time finding his rhythm. And he was tired.

Roy and Gaby reached his ball and looked down at the green from where his ball lay. The largest green on the course at nearly 7700 square feet with several subtle undulations resulted in numerous hole locations. The flag was on a small shelf on the right front section of the green, a tiny target if attempting to get the ball close. But even a conservative shot to the middle of the green made a three-putt a distinct possibility given the contours. Roy had played the course enough times to know that par would be a good score due to the hole location. And like all of the greens at Crystal Downs, almost every hole location created one place you could not hit it and have a reasonable chance to save par. With today's flag location, Roy knew that spot was short and right.

Roy aimed his 5-iron at the middle of the green and hoped to let his putter do the rest. His misses left on #2, #4 and #6 nagged at his subconscious and he held on a bit too tight, sending his ball short and right of the green.

A huge mistake, making the likely result bogey or worse.

Ed knew he had a chance to extend his lead and played his 8-iron to the middle of the green leaving himself a 20-footer for birdie. Still not an easy putt but with Roy in trouble, a good play.

Roy stood over his ball in the rough short of the green considering his options while staring at the flag on the tiny shelf just 10 yards in front of him. He could try to land his chip in the rough and hope that took enough speed off it while still releasing onto the green. But if his ball stayed in the rough, he'd most likely lose the hole. He could play a safe shot onto the green and hope to sink a long, difficult putt. Or, there was one other option...

Earlier that year, Roy, Ed and Fred had traveled to Indian Wells, California to escape the Michigan winter for a week of golf. During their visit, Roy found a 64-degree lob wedge at Pete Carlson's Golf Shop and was instantly fascinated by it. Roy's always loved hitting aggressive shots and experimenting with ways out of difficult situations. Both Ed and Fred had tried to talk him out of buying the 64-degree wedge, noting that even among the best players in the world, very few carried one. Roy bought the club anyway and used it throughout the week, eliciting howls of laughter from his playing partners as every shot he attempted with it went straight up in the air and back down, rarely advancing more than a few feet forward. Undeterred, he had kept the club in his bag and spent the spring and summer having fun practicing with it.

And now Roy had the shot and the club that the moment called for. He reached into his bag and pulled the 64-degree wedge.

Ed leaned on his putter near where his ball was marked on the green and watched, curious as to how his dad would play the near-impossible shot.

Addressing the ball, Roy told himself to feel the distance to the hole. He took a fluid, wonderfully lazy swing and his ball flew straight up in the air then straight down like a badminton birdie, landing with a soft thud. His ball barely rolled an inch after landing, finishing three inches from the hole.

Ed's mouth hung open as he stared dumbfounded at the ball next to the hole.

The tables had turned.

Ed now faced a tricky two-putt to halve the hole. He had to hit it hard enough to get the ball up on the shelf but soft enough to avoid running it past the hole where the green sloped away. He stroked it towards the hole…the ball climbed the shelf, slowed and settled four feet short. A decent effort but not within the range of a concession. Roy watched Ed survey his remaining four-footer that had a degree of break near the hole. His line needed to be perfect or the putt would slip by. Ed stroked the putt and it appeared to be going in the left-center of the hole when it suddenly spun out, hanging on the lip. Ed stared at the ball in disbelief as Roy thanked his 64-degree wedge for the win.

All-Square through six holes.

26

Hole #7 - 335 Yards - Par 4

Standing on the 7th tee, Roy felt a jolt of adrenaline run through his veins. He'd survived the first six holes with a mix of luck and determination and had turned a potential 2-Down deficit into an even match. His tension and concern about his poor swings faded, replaced by a desire and eagerness to hit his next shot.

The 7th is wonderfully unique. The straight and plateaued fairway slopes slightly downhill with fescue bordering the left side. You can lay-up on top of the plateau, leaving a short iron downhill to a one-of-a-kind boomerang-shaped green that appears to rest in a punch bowl. Or you can try to hit driver down the hill, hoping to avoid the fescue and hazard on the left and leave a short blind wedge over a crest back up to the green.

Buoyed by his par-save, Roy took the aggressive route and ripped his driver. He didn't have to ask Gaby where it went. Straight and true.

Ed followed with a perfect drive of his own.

Heading down the fairway, Ed and Roy felt the intensity of the match ratchet up a notch. Ed sensed his dad had weathered the early storm and his confidence was back; Roy's experience told him Ed's focus and intensity were ramping up and better shots were coming.

"You know, Pa, it's a shame there aren't a few people out here watching. This is turning into a good match and there are some pretty good shots being hit. Or in your case, I should say some interesting shots."

"You know, Ed, it's Sunday and people have things going on with their families. They aren't interested in watching me kick your butt."

The match was on.

Both Roy and Ed had about 80-yard shots left to the green. The only key was making sure they landed on the same half of the boomerang where the flag was located. Both did and easily two-putted for par.

All-Square through seven holes.

27

Hole #8 - 550 Yards - Par 5

The magnificent and difficult 8th hole is also listed by *Golf Magazine* as one of the Top 100 holes in the world and widely acclaimed as one of the best par fives in golf. On no other hole is it more evident that Crystal Downs was built before the advent of powerful earth-moving equipment—the hole's contours shaped by nature, a pond sledge and team of mules.

The hole climbs uphill from the tee, a slight dogleg-right to the treacherous green in the distance, perched high on a ledge. Fescue guards the right and left of the entire hole with a large tree blocking shots hit off the tee into the fescue on the right. Even drives landing in the fairway are at the mercy of the undulating knobs and knolls, leaving unpredictable and uneven lies.

Roy and Ed both hit excellent drives. Arriving in the fairway, each faced fairway wood shots from slightly uneven lies. They each striped 3-woods up the right side of the fairway, Ed carrying his shot 10-to-15-yards past Roy.

The approach shot to the elevated 8th green requires precision. If the shot doesn't carry deep enough into the green past the false front, it will trickle back to the front of the green and then tumble down the hill over 30 yards. As a result, the approach often creates anxiety and frustration for a player after hitting an apparently good shot onto the green that disappears for a moment only to reappear, rolling back as the golfer helplessly watches what appeared to be a birdie putt turn into a tricky uphill pitch shot.

Roy knew the key was to hit his approach deep enough into the green so it held but without hitting it too long—long was dead. He hit a crisp 7-iron that landed on the left side of the green, disappearing from view…and after a few anxious seconds when the ball didn't reappear, he knew it had settled on the green.

Ed hit a perfect three-quarter 9-iron to keep the spin down and left himself an eight-footer for birdie.

Arriving at the green, Roy discovered the challenging putt awaiting him. Twenty feet with as much as two-to-three feet of break. Despite the degree of difficulty, he didn't spend much time studying the putt.

Trust your first impression. Pick the line. Stroke it.

Roy's putt tracked along the slope, turned for the hole and dropped dead-center! Birdie four. Undaunted and relishing the pressure, Ed stepped up and drained his eight-foot birdie right on top of his dad's.

All-Square after eight holes.

28

Hole #9 - 175 Yards - Par 3

The challenging 9th plays uphill to a green perched 30 feet above the tee framed by the pro shop behind it. The green slopes severely back-to-front with a large bunker protecting the right side and the left side dropping off steeply down a fescue-covered hill. Legend has it, after drawing the layout of the golf course, MacKenzie sat down with his associate, Perry Maxwell, on the site of what is now the 9th green. Unrolling the paper, he showed him the layout, declaring it one of his best designs. After pondering the plans for a few moments, Maxwell told MacKenzie he loved it except for one small problem: there were only 17 holes. Furious, MacKenzie grabbed the document and looked at it for several moments. Cursing, he stood up, looked around, took a pencil from his shirt pocket and in a matter of minutes designed the 9th hole.

As Roy and Ed approached the tee, they noticed several people gathered above the green in front of the pro shop. Both

Roy and Ed stayed focused, mindful of the risks on the 9th and played shots short of the hole—Ed ended up on the front of the green and Roy just short of the putting surface. Roy chipped up close and they both made pars, eliciting polite applause from their growing gallery.

The Championship was All-Square after nine holes.

29

The Turn

As Roy and Ed walked up the hill from the 9th green, they found a crowd of people had gathered around the 10th tee. Word had spread that the match was close and the banter and laughter of members and their children filled the air.

Roy was beloved by his fellow members and the staff at Crystal Downs. He greeted everyone with a smile and always had time to stop to chat and listen. He especially loved hanging out with the caddies who affectionately referred to him as "Dr. Roy." Almost all who had come to know him well had their favorite "Roy Story." For some, it was a random act of kindness or generosity—Roy had driven over six hours round-trip on more than one occasion to pick someone up from Detroit Metro Airport. For others, their favorite "Roy Story" took on a more humorous slant. Even if they hadn't personally been involved, Roy's friends loved earning the laughs from retelling them.

There was the Florida Car Story. Roy's always had a weak

spot for used cars, van and motor homes. One time, he flew commercially down to Florida with his two oldest sons to fish and play some golf. While in Key West, Roy decided to go look at cars for fun. He found a deal he couldn't pass up, bought a used car right off the lot, cancelled their return flights and they drove the 1700 miles home.

The Arizona Lumber Story. Roy and three friends from Crystal Downs were in Phoenix one winter on a golf trip. Driving from their hotel to the golf course, Roy looked out at the barren desert and wondered aloud, "When do you suppose they lumbered this off?"

That Royism would do Yogi Berra proud and is fittingly topped by The Lou Gehrig Story. A big storm front blew through Crystal Downs one fall afternoon and everyone was pulled off the golf course. Several guys were sitting around Fred's desk in his office telling stories. It was during the World Series and they got on the topic of who was the best player who ever lived. One guy said Babe Ruth, another said Mickey Mantle, then someone said Lou Gehrig to which Roy said, "Yeah, Lou Gehrig was a great player...is he still alive?" Fred shook his head in disbelief, "Roy, come on. He died a tragic early death of Lou Gehrig's disease." To which Roy replied, "Gosh, what do you think the odds of that were?"

The Fishing Bag Story. Roy, Ed, and Ed's wife, Tam, were flying out of Traverse City Airport. Roy hates being late for anything—he's often as much as an hour early for an appointment—but in this case he was running behind and grabbed his bag from his van and tossed some things in. When the TSA employee opened his bag, she said, "Oh, we have a lot of problems here." First, she took out a spark-plug wrench with all of the sockets. Then she took out a 9" filet knife. She was on her radio in a flash and the next thing Roy knew, security had him surrounded. Roy innocently explained that he'd forgotten what was in the bag and he'd just go put it back in the car. Before he could move, security stopped him and told him he wasn't going anywhere. In Roy's haste, he had grabbed his fishing bag instead of his duffle bag. Airport security called the city cops who filed a police report and when Roy got back in town, he had to meet with the prosecuting attorney who was able to get the charges dropped.

Roy had another run-in with law enforcement and emergency responders in The Hot Tub Story. A few years back in the middle of winter, Roy was home alone and decided to change the water in the hot tub outside his home. The circuit breaker to turn off the electricity was underneath the deck and Roy crawled below to turn if off so he could drain the hot tub. But Roy got stuck beneath the deck. Couldn't move forward or back. He started shouting for help but no one could hear him. Fortunately, he had his cell phone with him, was able to reach it and dial 911. Next thing he knew, a fire engine, ambulance and a couple of sheriffs' cars rolled into his neighborhood looking for him. Dispatch was still on the phone with him, trying to figure out which house was his to which Roy responded, "I'm the one with the guy with his legs sticking out from underneath the deck!"

Stories like these combined with his golfing prowess had made Roy a living legend among his fellow members. And when word spread that Roy was making a match out of it on the front nine, his friends pulled away from their activities on that summer Sunday afternoon, grabbed their families and headed up to the club to bear witness in case something magical happened and Roy pulled off the improbable…

30

Hole #10 - 395 Yards - Par 4

The 10th tee is one of the great awe-inspiring spots in golf. The back edge of the tee starts right up against the pro shop and a large window a few paces behind the tee markers provides a wonderful vantage point to watch golfers tee off. Standing on the elevated tee, you can see most of the front nine to your right. Crystal Lake shimmers in the distance beyond the golf course, while below you can see members practicing on the simple driving range. Down and off to the left, the 18th tee's cut into the hillside, a reminder of where you're working towards. Straight in front of the tee and steeply down, the fairway—the task at hand. Fescue guards the right and left of the fairway that climbs back up to the elevated green.

Never one to shy from an audience, Roy launched his driver long and down the middle. The ball hung in the air forever, appearing like it might fly all the way to the green before dropping into the fairway. The gallery applauded as Ed stepped up and matched Roy's wonderful drive with one of his own.

While Roy and Ed surveyed their shots in the fairway, the gallery continued up the hill to get a better view of the second shots. The approach to the 10th green requires a carry over a pot bunker onto a putting surface that slopes severely back-to-front and left-to-right. Bunkers and fescue guard the left side. The right side falls off down the hill. Leave it short and you'll come back down the hill or end up in the bunker. Long and left are both dead.

Roy sized up his shot—135 yards to a middle hole location. Factoring in the uphill, he aimed his 7-iron left of the flag and hit it where he wanted. The gallery began shouting and applauding as his ball came to rest. One of the members held up his hands five inches apart—Roy had knocked it stiff!

Ed knew he had to make a birdie to halve and aimed his 9-iron just left of the hole but his ball landed short, rolled back, and came to rest on the fringe. As the gallery gathered to watch Ed try to make his putt to tie, Fred noticed his two assistant professionals, Andy Bell and Brian Sleeman, standing among the members.

"Guys, who's manning the shop?" Fred asked.

"Fred, we gotta see this!" Brian exclaimed.

Ed's putt rolled up the hill and broke right as it crested, tracking towards the hole then kept breaking and missed by a few inches.

Up until that point in the match, Fred figured there was no way Roy could win. He'd thought back to the last time Roy won the Club Championship, 11 years ago in 1999 when Roy was 67. It had seemed like a miracle at the time, something Fred was sure he'd never witness again. At 78, Roy was too old. It was too much golf over three days. Ed was too good. It might be a fun match for a while then Ed would pull away.

But for the first time that day, a thought crept into Fred's head.

Roy could win this thing.

Roy was 1-Up with eight holes left to play.

31

Hole #11 - 196 Yards - Par 3

Diabolical. That's the nicest way to describe the 11th that marks the beginning of a stretch of holes with a different feel than the first ten. Trees line the entire hole creating a chute from the tee box. The 196 yards, all-carry, play longer on account of the green resting 26 feet above the tee. Despite the elevation change, you can see the entire putting surface from the tee box indicating how severe the slope of the green is from back-to-front. Bunkers guard the green left and long. And adding to the difficulty, the green has three distinct levels. A ball hit past the correct tier often leads to a putt off the green. Even a shot hit into the green will run all the way back down off the green and 30 yards down the hill if it catches the wrong slope.

Roy aimed his hybrid at the hole cut on the first level of the green but hit his shot slightly short and right of the green and his ball held up in the light rough. Ed followed with a wonderful shot that settled 12 feet from the flag.

Roy knew to get his chip close, he needed to use the slope. He played his shot so it ran slightly up the hill and the gallery started cheering as his ball trickled back down to the hole and finished inside a foot for a conceded par. The severity of the green meant Ed couldn't be too aggressive and he lagged his putt close for a par of his own.

The gallery had introduced a new dynamic. While both Roy and Ed had parred the hole, Roy's chip had required a little flair and entertained the gallery more than Ed's routine two-putt. The cheers from Roy's approach into #10 and his chip on #11 also left no question, to the surprise of no one, for whom the gallery was rooting.

Roy remained 1-Up with seven holes left to play.

32

Hole #12 - 430 Yards - Par 4

The dogleg-right 12th presents the most difficult driving hole on the course. Fescue runs the entire left side of the fairway. The right side's bordered by fescue then trees and finally a road, out-of-bounds. A giant beech tree straight off the tee appears to provide an aiming point but the tree actually stands in the left rough. The play is to cut a drive off the tree or hit a straight shot that hugs the inside of the right tree line as the fairway opens up slightly on the right, out of view.

Roy overswung and his shot bounded left into the rough making a hard hole even harder. Ed knew he had an opening and responded with a perfect fade off the right edge of the beech tree that came to rest in the middle of the fairway, leaving himself a mid-to-short iron to the green.

Roy's ball was settled in the rough, about 210 yards away, stymied by the beech tree. With no chance to reach the green from his lie, he knew he had to give himself a chance to scramble for par so he punched a 7-iron, chasing the ball down the fairway 50 yards short of the green.

The 12th green is different than most at Crystal Downs in that the slightly elevated surface slants from front-to-back. Ed took less club, factoring in the helping wind and green running away from him. His 8-iron flew true and finished 18 feet from the hole.

Roy had a good lie in the fairway short of the green and just wanted to give himself a good putt for par. He clipped it cleanly—too cleanly—and rather than releasing on the green, his ball checked up 15 feet short of the hole.

Ed could win the hole and even-up the match if he drained his birdie putt but Fred's hole locations for the Championship Sunday took advantage of the subtleties and challenges of the greens. If Ed got too aggressive, he'd run it by so he opted to lag it close for a conceded par.

Roy faced a must-make for the first time since the 4th hole and didn't want to surrender his 1-Up lead nor let the momentum shift to Ed. He picked his line and let it roll...end-over-end...dead-center!

The gallery cheered as Roy pulled his ball out of the hole. Ed shook his head after another one of his dad's trademark scrambling pars while Roy smiled at his lucky ball—so far good for 15 putts through 12 holes.

Roy was 1-Up with six holes left to play.

33

Hole #13 - 442 Yards - Par 4

Considered the most difficult hole to par on the course, the 13th completes the brutally tough four-hole start to the back nine. A gentle dogleg left-to-right with a fairway that slopes hard left-to-right. Trees line the entire right side. Rough and fescue protects the left.

Roy ripped a perfect drive up the left side that caught the slope, bounced right and bounded forward, rolling considerably before it stopped.

Roy smiled at his son, "Ed, I don't want to see you hurt yourself trying to catch that."

"Great. Now I've got my 78-year-old dad trash-talking me," Ed muttered as he bent down to tee his ball up.

Reaching back for a little extra, Ed cracked a perfect drive up the left side of the fairway that bounded forward like Roy's. Everyone watched from the tee as it appeared to stop a few yards shy of Roy's ball, leaving Roy grinning ear-to-ear.

Two wonderful drives were just the down payment on the 13th. The exceptionally difficult green features a tiny crowned front portion that drops off to a larger rear section sloping dramatically from left-to-right. Bunkers protect the green on both sides with the front right falling off to a bunker below the green.

The back hole location called for a shot to carry the ridge in the middle of the green but also meant that the approach shots likely wouldn't hold. Better to be long and chipping back up to the hole than trying to stop the ball on the green and ending up on the front having to putt down the slope.

Ed knew his 165-yard shot would play closer to 180. He hit a 5-iron at the left-center that carried the ridge, landed on the green and hopped right. Even though it wouldn't stay on the green, Ed was confident he'd get up and down for par.

Roy faced an identical shot and hit a carbon copy. He couldn't see where his shot finished but figured it'd be close to Ed's. Even though both players had missed the green, the gallery applauded, recognizing the difficulty of the hole.

As expected, their balls ended up only a couple of feet apart in the light rough just off the edge of the green. Roy and Ed each hit routine uphill chips close for par.

Roy had played the demanding 10th-through-13th in 1-under par while Ed had played it even par. Roy was even par for the match with only 16 putts in 13 holes, Ed was 2-over par due to his double-bogey on the 1st.

And Roy was still 1-Up with five holes left to play.

34

Hole #14 - 147 Yards - Par 3

The beautiful 14th offers a chance to take a quick breath and regroup. Nestled in a scenic setting, bunkers front, right and left protect the back-to-front sloping green. A deeply sloping hill covered with ferns and greens stretches out behind the green providing a spectacular vista of the Empire Bay of Lake Michigan and majestic Sleeping Bear Dunes in the distance. The combination of surrounding trees and open land tend to create a swirling wind and any shot missing the green leaves hard work for par.

Both Roy and Ed hit short irons on the green, Roy's landing in the middle of the green and Ed's right-center then trickling to the edge. They both two-putted easily and walked off the farthest spot on the back nine from the clubhouse to start the march towards home.

Roy remained 1-Up with four holes left to play.

35

Hole #15 - 327 Yards - Par 4

The 15th's aptly nicknamed "Little Poison." At first glance from the tee, the hole looks straightforward. Fescue on both sides of what appears to be a generous fairway. Large fairway bunker right with woods behind it. Another bunker slightly farther, left of the fairway. The elevated, subtly crowned green protected by bunkers front left and right. The premium is on accuracy not distance on the short par four as the fairway narrows the longer you hit it but anything shorter than a 230-yard drive leaves a blind second shot due to the undulating fairway.

The hole was playing back into the wind and Roy knew that over the years Ed had made as many birdies on #15 as any other hole on the course. Roy caught his drive slightly off-center and pulled it left, turning anxiously to Gaby tracking the ball bouncing toward the fescue.

"Where'd it go?"

"Left, toward the fescue but I think it stopped short."

Ed hit a draw into the wind to try and get some run out of it but pulled it a bit from where he was aiming. His ball hit the fairway and bounced left, settling in the first cut of rough.

Roy anxiously approached his ball, hoping for a good lie. Gaby's eagle eyes had proved correct—his ball was in the rough just short of the fescue. With the hole middle-left he also had a good angle for his 115-yard approach with the wind and elevated green stretching his shot closer to 135-140 yards. Fall-offs short and left of the green combined with subtle contours on the putting surface seemed to repel approach shots landing anywhere but the center.

Roy hit his 8-iron just right of the flag and loved his shot the moment he struck it. His excitement quickly shifted to anxiety as his ball drifted left in the wind and landed a few feet from where he was aiming on the green, rolled left off the green and settled in the rough. Not a disaster but he'd gone from thinking he had a birdie chance while his ball was mid-flight to facing an up-and-down for par.

Ed also had a good lie in the rough and took dead-aim with his 9-iron. His ball tracked just right of the flag, dropped and stopped eight feet from the hole. The gallery cheered in appreciation.

Roy didn't waste any time with his chip and knocked it close for a conceded par then stepped aside and watched Ed examining his line. Roy knew what was coming and steeled himself for the final three holes as Ed's putt rolled dead-center. Six-inches from the cup, Ed started walking after it then stopped mid-stride as his ball veered offline at the last moment, caught the lip and spun out.

Little Poison.

Roy was still 1-Up with only three holes left to play!

36

Hole #16 - 588 Yards - Par 5

The gallery had grown and was buzzing as Roy and Ed approached the 16th tee of the second and last par five on the course. A slight dogleg right-to-left with fescue bordering both sides of the fairway, the first half of the hole played moderately uphill and today was directly into the wind.

Roy knew it would take him three solid shots to get home and reminded himself to play one at a time starting with the drive. At the last moment, he tried to give it a little extra into the wind. He turned quickly toward Gaby.

"Left?"

"Yeah," she said, intently following the ball's flight into the fescue.

Seeing Roy's tired swing, Fred feared his friend was starting to wear out and wondered if he'd be able to hold off the inevitable charge from Ed.

Roy knew he'd given Ed an opening and watched as Ed

smacked his tee shot hard up the right side. Ed's ball landed on the edge of the fairway and hopped into the first cut of rough. He'd be in good shape while Roy was facing either a lost ball or a pitch out.

Gaby had smartly picked a mark where she thought Roy's ball landed and quickly found it. Amazingly, the lucky ball had come to rest almost teed up in a patch of very thin fescue. The flier lie meant Roy could get a fairway wood on the ball without much risk. He ripped his 3-wood and the gallery cheered as his ball flew down the middle of the fairway. A spectacular recovery but still over 200 yards remained for his third shot.

Ed hadn't seen the lie, just the surprise of his dad swinging 3-wood and his ball sailing out of the fescue. Ed knew Roy would have to work hard for his par and he liked his odds as he approached his ball in the rough.

One of the great charms of golf is summed up in four words. Rub of the Green. Golfers experience it in every round. One ball rockets off a tree back into play, another nicks a hanging leaf and is never found again. A good lie here, bad lie there. Good kicks, bad bounces. And while golfers are responsible for monitoring and enforcing the rules, The Golf Gods administer the Rub of the Green. And those Golf Gods appear unpredictably, sometimes punishing good shots, other times rewarding bad ones, appearing to play favorites one moment, then just as quickly dropping one player for another.

After Roy's shot, Ed walked toward his ball thinking about how he would play his next shot. The second shot on #16 didn't call for any heroics. Trees and rough right, fescue left. A fairway wood or hybrid hit solidly would leave a short iron to the green.

As Ed reached his ball in the rough, his stomach dropped.

His ball had settled into an awful lie in a spot of rough growing against the ball, significantly thicker than the grass around it. He'd only missed the fairway by a few feet and faced an almost unplayable lie. Reaching the green in three shots was out of the question. He'd have to scramble for par.

Roy watched Ed hack his ball out, advancing it only 60 yards down the fairway. Still away, Ed smoked his next shot with his 3-wood straight at the green, coming up about 40 yards short.

Roy stood over his ball, about 210 yards from a right-center flag, playing into a strong breeze. The green sloped back-to-front with a few different shelves guarded by bunkers front and left. Like all the greens at Crystal Downs, it was essential to be on the correct shelf.

Calculating the carry and the wind, Roy figured it would play 225 yards. Perfect distance for his 5-wood.

A few months earlier, while on a shopping trip with Shirley in Grand Rapids, Roy had wandered into a Dick's Sporting Goods and bought a Walter Hagen 5-wood on sale. Roy hadn't bothered hitting it first. Didn't get custom-fit or test it on a launch monitor. He liked the way it looked. And he had an affinity for its namesake.

Walter Hagen won the Michigan Open in 1921 and the Michigan PGA in 1930 and 1931, all before Roy was born. Hagen went on to win 11 major championships, third most in history, which doesn't include five victories in the Western Open—essentially a major at that time—and not playing in The Masters until the end of his career. Hagen's legacy of golf extends to this day. He helped found The PGA of America and co-founded The Ryder Cup, captaining the team six straight times. He retired from golf in 1939 with 75 career victories and lived out the end of his days not far from Crystal Downs on Long Lake where he made his home until he died in 1969. Almost 100 years since Hagen played in the same 1913 U.S. Open where Francis Ouimet became the first amateur to win and catapulted the game into the public consciousness, his legend lived on as a sporting brand.

So it wasn't just any club that had caught Roy's eye that day.

He pulled the Hagen 5-wood out of his bag.

Took his stance. Took a deep breath to calm himself. And took dead-aim.

He knew it was true the second it left the club. Gaby watched his ball sail towards the green…land, roll right and stop 10 feet from the hole.

The gallery erupted.

From a possible lost tee shot to a putt for birdie.

Roy watched Ed, knowing he'd put the pressure on him to get his tricky 40-yard wedge shot close. If Ed tried to get too cute and missed short or left, his ball could come back off the green. Undeterred, Ed hit a solid pitch 10 feet from the hole.

Rather than make a run at birdie, Roy lagged his putt close for a conceded and unlikely par. He then stepped out of the way to watch Ed face his first must-make putt since the 10th hole. Roy knew Ed thrived on the competition and for moments like this and fully expected him to make it despite having 18 inches of break. Ed's putt rolled towards the apex and took the break directly towards the hole. Roy and the gallery watched with anticipation as the ball slid towards the edge of the hole, started to curl in and somehow stayed out, finishing directly behind the hole.

The Golf Gods had struck again.

Roy was 2-Up with two holes to play!

37

Hole #17 - 311 Yards - Par 4

Described by Michigan Golf Hall of Fame member Lynn Janson as "Three hundred and eleven yards of sheer terror," the 17th is a visually breathtaking, unusual golf hole. The tiny elevated tee sits high above the narrow, tree-lined fairway. Lake Michigan shimmers in the distant horizon beyond the green which is perched on a tiny plateau almost level with the tee but high above the fairway. Regardless of club selection, the 17th demands a precise shot down to the uneven, serpentine fairway and even a good drive tends to leave an uneven lie back uphill to the elevated green.

Playing in his usual fearless childlike fashion, Roy often hit driver on the 17th, ripping it into the narrow landing area just short of the green. But with so much on the line, needing only to halve the hole to secure the championship, the prudent play was conservative. Get the ball in play, put the pressure on Ed. So Roy reached in his bag...and grabbed his driver.

The gallery hushed as Roy addressed the ball, steadied and swung. His drive bore through the stiff wind, straight down the middle...landed, bounced left and up the fairway slope before rolling back 20 yards and settling in the light rough about 80 yards short and below the green.

Ed had no margin of error—he had to win the hole to continue the match. He steeled himself and smacked his hybrid down the middle, his ball coming to rest in the fairway about 110 yards from the hole.

The players moved out, gallery in tow, with the championship hanging in the balance and tilting improbably toward Roy.

The approach shot into the 17th green is notoriously difficult from a typically uneven lie up to the false-front green with bunkers right and left. Long is dead and anything short rolls 40 yards off the green back down the hill. The wind often blows in unobstructed over the green, adding to the challenge.

Factoring in the wind and elevation, Ed hit his 7-iron just right of the flag in the middle of the green, his ball rolling to a stop about 10 feet from the hole.

The gallery applauded his wonderful shot under pressure.

Roy knew he controlled his destiny. Birdie the hole and it was over. Make par and force Ed to make birdie to extend it.

Roy pulled his 8-iron and addressed the ball as the gallery grew still around him. He started his backswing and as Roy rotated back towards the ball, his arms collapsed, the club visibly decelerating. His clubhead thudded into the ground and the ball flew left and low disappearing into the high fescue 30 yards away.

The gallery gasped as Roy hung his head. His tank had abruptly hit empty—nerves and exhaustion overwhelming the adrenaline that had been pushing him along.

Standing at the edge of the gallery, Fred put his hand over his mouth and looked down. *Don't run out of gas. Not now. Please not now*, thought Fred.

The gallery helped Roy look for his ball and quickly found it in a terrible lie. Roy futilely tried to gouge it out with a wedge but was barely able to get it airborne and his ball disappeared again into the heavy fescue.

Everyone joined in another search but it was fruitless and Roy conceded the hole to Ed.

As the gallery moved on, Roy walked slowly through the high fescue grass desperately searching for his golf ball that he'd played for 31 holes starting with the first hole of his semi-finals match that morning.

Roy trudged through the rough, exhausted from playing six rounds in three days, hoping to find a flash of white hidden in the thick, tangled grass. Hoping for one more miracle.

It wasn't to be.

He gave up the search and headed towards the 18th tee.

Roy was 1-Up with one hole left to play in the Championship.

And he had lost his lucky ball.

Whatever may be a player's skill, he must
have luck to win a championship of any
kind, at least he must have no bad luck;
golf is still a game rather than a science,
and a game it is likely to remain.
– Bobby Jones

Luck is the zest of life, as well as golf.
– Dr. Alister MacKenzie

38

Hole #18 - 400 Yards - Par 4

The elevated 18th championship tee sits alone shaped into the hillside below the back of the 17th green and above the 10th green. Fescue lines the entire right and inside of the dogleg left-to-right as well as the left side of the fairway. The classic clubhouse perches high on the hill straight away overlooking the finishing hole, an American Flag atop a pole, waving in the wind.

The angle of the dogleg makes it key to pick the correct line off the tee. A straight drive can run through the fairway into the rough and fescue beyond. A drive that cuts off too much of the right corner won't clear the fescue.

Roy tried to regroup as he approached the tee, hoping for a final burst of energy. All he had to do was tie the hole and the championship was his. But his head felt cloudy, his body weak and tired.

Ed prepared to tee off, his mind clear and sharp. He knew his dad was rattled and felt if he could hit a good tee shot, he could keep the pressure on. Win #18 to tie the match then close him out in extra holes. 78-year-olds don't win club championships. Certainly not on one of the top courses in the world. And certainly not against the best player in the club.

While Ed was teeing up his ball, Roy heard a commotion from their right.

"I found it!"

Damien Esterhuizen, a staff member of Crystal Downs who loved Roy, had stayed behind searching for the lost ball. He knew Roy's mindset when he had a lucky ball and he figured he had a few minutes to try and find it before Roy teed off the 18th. Damien ran down the path through the gallery to the tee and handed Roy his lucky #2 Titleist NXT while Ed shook his head, knowing that if he weren't witnessing it himself, he might not believe it.

Roy thanked Damien and grinned as he squeezed his lucky ball, a surge of adrenaline racing through his veins while Ed prepared to tee off.

The strong southwest wind created an additional challenge for the tee shot. Anything hit with a fade would likely ride the wind into the fescue on the right and Ed knew he had to start his drive left-center to compensate. He swung and his drive flew down the right side toward the corner of the dogleg...a bit farther right than intended and drifting in the wind...

His ball landed in the fescue and disappeared from sight.

Roy took a deep breath, calming his nerves, anxious to capitalize on Ed's mistake. He teed up his lucky ball and picked his target in the fairway.

Make par, force him to make birdie from the rough to win the hole.

Roy swung and came up out of it. He quickly turned to Gaby, "Did it go right?"

"Yeah, it's in the fescue."

Anything was possible for both of their balls. Lost, unplayable, decent lies. It was in The Golf Gods' hands.

Both Roy and Ed fortunately found their wayward shots. Roy's lie was decent but not good enough for him to reach the green. He needed to carefully consider his options but his mind was tired...then suddenly, the clouds cleared.

Don't try a miracle shot, just get it back in the fairway as close to the green as possible. Then get it up-and-down like you have all day. Just get the putter in your hands one more time.

Roy pitched out safely with his wedge, the ball coming to rest 20 yards short of the green.

Ed faced a different challenge. The 18th green sits tucked into the side of a hill surrounded by bunkers and fescue. From Ed's line, anything short, right or long would be in trouble. Anything left would kick down the false front. His poor lie made reaching the green risky and unlikely but winning the hole was his only way to force extra holes. He couldn't rely on his dad to mess up like he had on #17 and given Roy's outstanding putting all day, Ed was compelled to play a more aggressive shot. His only chance of getting the ball airborne out of the lie was to rip through the tangled grass so he took a strong, wide stance and tried to swing his 7-iron as hard as he could. It wasn't enough. Ed's ball travelled barely 30 yards forward, staying in the fescue

Roy watched from the fairway as Ed walked through the fescue and located his ball. Roy knew Ed wouldn't let up, would never throw in the towel. His son was likely thinking he could pull off a miracle hole-out or at the worst knock it close and still save par.

Ed ripped his wedge, managing to dig the ball out of the

gnarly lie. His ball flew high and straight at the flag, dropped down and rolled to a stop eight feet from the hole.

The gallery cheered the magnificent recovery. Ed was still alive.

But Roy was in control of his destiny. Get up-and-down for par and it would be over.

Roy surveyed his 20-yard pitch shot which was anything but routine. He had to carry the ball up to the slightly elevated green and past the false front. Anything short would roll back to him.

The gallery quieted as Roy pulled his sand wedge and set up for the shot.

Wasting no time, Roy swung and struck it cleanly—the ball landed on the green and stopped 15 feet below the hole.

The gallery cheered as Gaby handed Roy his putter and he walked up onto the green.

Eighteen holes of stroke play to qualify. Three matches to reach the final. After 17 holes in the final match, the club championship came down to two putts. If Roy made his 15-footer, it was over. If Roy missed and Ed made his eight-footer, the match was going to a sudden-death playoff starting back on the 1st hole.

The gallery fell silent as Roy studied the green. He loved putting more than any part of golf. Loved getting lost in his own world while playing the game within the game. And he was lost in that world now.

The putt wasn't easy. If he ran it past, he'd face a tricky downhill/sidehill come-backer.

Roy looked from his ball to the hole...

"There's the line. Right there," he said quietly to himself.

His stroke was pure, his ball rolled perfectly off the putter...

Three feet from the hole, it started breaking...

And like a gopher going down its hole—Roy's lucky ball dove into the center of the cup!

The gallery cheered as Ed walked across the green and embraced his victorious dad, Crystal Downs' 2010 Club Champion.

And the applause continued while Roy humbly tipped his hat and acknowledged his friends and fellow members.

Roy and Ed had both played stellar rounds, posting scores of two-over par in winds of 20 mph. The difference had been Roy's lucky ball—and 22 putts on the 17 holes he completed.

As the gallery dispersed, energized by what they'd witnessed, Fred congratulated Roy and Ed then quietly made his way back to the pro shop. Heading slowly up the hill, he was overwhelmed by the gifts of the day…his 25-year friendship with Roy, the beauty of the game, the magic of Crystal Downs…

Back in the pro shop, Fred closed the door to his office and sat down at his desk as tears of joy streamed down his face.

Epilogue: Living The Dream

Roy kept his magical summer going by teaming up with his good friend, Pat Griffin, to win the Crystal Downs Governor's Cup in spite of them giving strokes to their opponents in every match of the difficult alternate shot tournament. Roy then pulled off the trifecta, capping off his summer by winning the Crystal Downs Senior Club Championship.

Perhaps if this story had happened in another era, a young Bob Jones upon hearing of such an accomplishment by a 78-year-old amateur might have cabled Roy, offered his congratulations and invited him to travel south for a game at his new club.

But that's not the era we live in. And what transpired on a summer Sunday afternoon in Northern Michigan was left to become lore in its own time.

One morning in September, a couple of months after his remarkable victory, Roy bumped into long-time Crystal Downs member Chuck Knight in the pro shop. Knight's the former CEO of Emerson Electric and a member of another Alister MacKenzie course about 1000 miles southeast of Crystal Downs Country Club.

"Roy, three championships in one year. That's pretty

impressive," Chuck said. "Sounds like that should be worth a trip to Augusta."

Roy's face lit up.

The boy from Escanaba, the kid from Detroit, the soldier from America, the doctor from McBain, the father of four, the grandfather of six, the lifelong amateur golfer and 78-year-old Crystal Downs Country Club Champion had just been invited to play Bobby Jones' & Dr. Alister MacKenzie's masterpiece, Augusta National Golf Club.

Seeds planted in 1932, sprouted in 2010.

Perhaps Bobby Jones sent that cable after all.

As Roy climbed into his old SCRATCH van and headed home from the club with visions of putting sidesaddle on Augusta's legendary greens filling his head, he smiled to himself...

Boy, am I lucky.

Afterword

Roy's still seeing patients, ripping his driver and draining putts.

He took a brief break from the game during the summer of 2012 after getting a pacemaker put in and was back playing by the fall.

Roy celebrated his 81st birthday by partnering with Ed in January of 2013 to win Tom Doak's Renaissance Cup contested at Doak's and Coore & Crenshaw's new courses at Streamsong in Florida.

He's looking forward to his next shot and his next round of golf.

About The Authors & Photographer

Brian & Roy

BRIAN MULVANEY

Brian grew up in Lansing, Michigan and graduated from Michigan State University with a B.A. in Psychology before earning a M.A. in Management from the Peter F. Drucker School of the Claremont Graduate University. He spent nearly twenty years with ARAMARK Corporation serving as

Executive Vice President of Administration as well as a member of the Executive Council and Presidents Council before retiring in 2004. Since then, Brian has focused on different business and charitable interests, foremost of which is The John L. Mulvaney Foundation which he founded with his wife, Kay, in 2000. The Foundation operates with an entrepreneurial approach assisting community-based charities serving people in extreme need, providing capital as well as planning and public relations services designed to extend the impact of these organizations. Brian is an avid golfer and emulated Roy's approach to the game in winning his first club championship in 2010. He splits his time between Southern California and Northern Michigan. Brian has always loved to write. *Roy: The 78-Year-Old Champion* is his first book.

mulvaneyfoundation.org

JAY LAVENDER

Jay was born in Albuquerque, New Mexico, grew up in Evanston, Illinois, and graduated from Dartmouth College where he played on the golf team. He moved to Los Angeles after graduation and worked as a driver and assistant until selling his first screenplay in 1999. Jay directed the call-to-action *Faster Vaccines* (2009) for the bipartisan Congressional Commission on the Prevention of Weapons of Mass Destruction Proliferation and Terrorism, blogged up Kilimanjaro with *Summit on the Summit* (2010), and directed and produced the short documentary film *Wounded Warriors' Resilience* (2011) that premiered at the 9/11 Tenth Anniversary Summit at The Newseum in Washington, DC and won the Audience Favorite Award for Best Documentary Short at the 2011 Virginia Film Festival. His film credits include *The Break-*

Up, The Fluffy Movie and *The Wedding Ringer*. Jay is an avid golfer and lives in Virginia. *Roy: The 78 Year-Old Champion is* his first book.

JayLavender.com
twitter.com/JayLavender
facebook.com/byJayLavender

DICKIE MORRIS

Sarah Dickinson "Dickie" Morris was born and raised in Charlottesville, Virginia and graduated from the University of Virginia. She has worked in event planning for the past eight years and is the owner of just a little ditty..., her lifestyle company she created to combine her passions: event planning, designing and sewing handmade ditty bags, photography and blogging. She also cofounded the event decor company, Stonegate Event Rentals, with her brother. Dickie and her ditty bags were featured in *Virginia Living Magazine* where she was named one of Virginia's Top Wedding Vendors for 2013.

justalittleditty.com
facebook.com/justalittleditty
instagram.com/justalittleditty

Dickie Morris, Jay Lavender, Roy Vomastek, Ed & Tam Vomastek

Photo Credits

1. High School Golf Team photo courtesy of Roy Vomastek
2. Roy Vomastek & Katsuaki Matsumoto photo courtesy of Roy Vomastek
3. Vomastek Family in Missouri photo courtesy of Roy Vomastek
4. McBain Presbyterian Church and Parsonage by Dickie Morris
5. Missaukee Golf Club Sign by Dickie Morris
6. Fred Muller by Brian Mulvaney
7. Roy's Golf Clubs by Dickie Morris
8. Roy's Examination Room by Dickie Morris
9. Dr. Roy by Dickie Morris
10. Roy's Arnold Palmer Memorabilia by Dickie Morris
11. Roy's Matsumoto Poster by Dickie Morris
12. Roy's Trophy Case by Dickie Morris
13. Roy Teeing Off #2 at Crystal Downs Country Club by Jay Lavender
14. Roy Putting On #4 at Crystal Downs Country Club by Dickie Morris
15. Roy & Gaby Muller by Dickie Morris
16. Roy's Van by Dickie Morris

17. Roy & Ed Vomastek by Dickie Morris
18. Roy's Final Putt #1 by Chuck Cox
19. Roy's Final Putt #2 by Chuck Cox
20. Roy's Final Putt #3 by Chuck Cox
21. Roy's Final Putt #4 by Chuck Cox
22. Roy & Ed's Hug by Chuck Cox
23. Roy's Lucky Ball by Dickie Morris
24. Roy On The 18th Tee at Crystal Downs Country Club by Dickie Morris
25. Brian Mulvaney & Roy by Jay Lavender
26. Dickie Morris, Jay Lavender, Roy, Ed & Tam Vomastek by Gaby Muller

For more information about *Roy*, NSPYR and updates on upcoming books & projects, sign up for our email list by emailing Fans@NSPYR.com as well as like, check & follow:

NSPYR.com
twitter.com/NSPYR
facebook.com/FueledByNSPYR

To order copies of *Roy* for your pro shop or to send correspondence to Dr. Roy Vomastek, please email Roy@NSPYR.com.

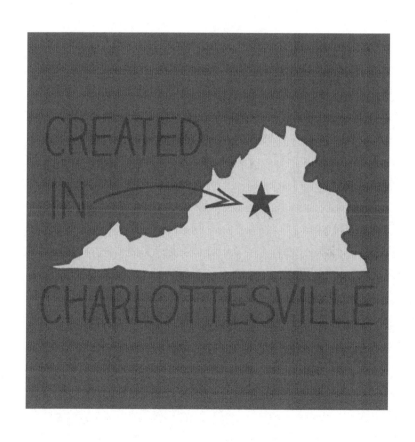

Made in the USA
Lexington, KY
14 October 2015